THE FINANCING OF FOREIGN DIRECT INVESTMENT

THE FINANCING OF FOREIGN DIRECT INVESTMENT:

A Study of the Determinants
of Capital Flows in
Multinational Enterprises

Martin G. Gilman

Preface by Charles P. Kindleberger

St. Martin's Press, New York

All rights reserved. For information, write:
St. Martin's Press, Inc., 175 Fifth Avenue, New York, NY 10010
Printed in Great Britain
First published in the United States of America in 1980

Library of Congress Cataloging in Publication Data

Gilman, Martin G
    The financing of foreign direct investment.

    Bibliography: p.
    1. Investments, Foreign.   2. Capital movements.
3. International business enterprises — Finance.
I. Title.
HG4538.G53   658.1'52   80-39898
ISBN 0-312-28982-0

In Memory of

Harry G. Johnson

whose encouragement during my graduate studies and advice in the early stages of this research inspired the direction, the form and whatever contribution that this study makes to our understanding of international capital movements.

CONTENTS

ACKNOWLEDGEMENTS

This book would not have been possible without the moral support of numerous friends and of my family, who encouraged me to persevere despite my own misgivings, as well as the advice from several fellow economists. In particular, I would like to thank Mark Casson, Max Steuer, and Malcolm Knight for their comments when this work began; and Marian Bond, Benjamin J. Cohen, Yusuke Horiguchi, Bernard Hugonnier, Charles Kindleberger, and Geoffrey Maynard for their advice at the latter stage. In addition I am grateful for the indulgence of my associates at the OECD and the use of its facilities. The data were kindly furnished through an agreement with the Bureau of Economic Analysis of the US Department of Commerce where Betty Barker was particularly helpful. Lastly, I owe a deep debt of gratitude to Meghnad Desai whose moral support and guidance were undoubtedly the main determinants of my efforts in finishing this research. The views expressed herein should not necessarily be construed to represent those held by the above parties and I alone bear the responsibility for any errors.

PREFACE

Intellectual progress is made by successive generations climbing over and standing upon the shoulders of the earlier. This is somewhat uncomfortable for those who form the base of these structures, but they welcome it in the interest of scientific advance as well as being reminded that they have done likewise to their predecessors.

In 1960 Stephen Hymer wrote a thesis at M.I.T. in which he suggested that the multinational corporation was nothing more than a domestic firm with foreign operations. Trying to push beyond this, I argued that there were three stages of sophistication with respect to foreign-exchange problems: (1) national firms with foreign operations who felt uncomfortable outside their own currency, and like a fish in water, unconscious of any exchange risk inside; (2) multinational corporations, that tried to be a good citizen of every country and were reluctant to take a short or long position in any currency of a country in which it operated; and (3) international corporations, which sought to maximize the world value of their assets wherever located and thus were prepared to go short of weak currencies, long of the strong, without regard to the location of assets or operations. The distinctions, which never caught on, were extensible to other functional aspects of a firm's operations, such as hiring, research, location of new plants, and the like.

Now comes Martin Gilman, an official of the OECD working on multinational enterprises, writing in his own capacity, to extend the analysis of international finance in the multinational corporation and to penetrate more deeply into it. His book, which began as a thesis at the London School of Economics, makes a notable addition to the growing literature on exchange risk in the multinational

corporation, a subject, moreover, that has grown in importance since the adoption of floating exchange rates in 1973.
His analysis and insights are strongly recommended to
scholars and to practitioners alike. Both markets are expanding, along with the numbers of the scholars who will one day
stand on Dr. Gilman's shoulders.

Charles P. Kindleberger
Massachusetts Institute of Technology

I INTRODUCTION

When asked to explain what determines the choice of currencies used to finance the overseas operations of domestic firms, it would appear that businessmen and international economists have been speaking almost two different languages. The communication gap has remained large – with economists assuming that exchange markets work costlessly and with businessmen viewing market costs as being prohibitively high. Economists have, in any case, applied relatively little research effort to the question and have generally relied on simplifying assumptions employed elsewhere in the literature on the optimization of financial portfolios. Businessmen, aware of the complexities of accounting rules, the impact of various fiscal regimes and the costs of hedging on their profits valued in home currency, in general have viewed foreign exchange risks as being very expensive to reduce and so have devised 'rules of thumb' in many cases to minimize their exposure. This book attempts to explain these two different perceptions and to provide a plausible explanation of the determinants of capital flows financing foreign direct investment that incorporates the main elements of both approaches.

In the course of financing their foreign operations, multinational enterprises[1] are involved in a decision-making process which determines the directions and magnitude of substantial flows of financial capital. These international capital movements by direct investors have not been adequately explained by portfolio adjustment theories which have been successfully applied to other aspects of the capital accounts of the balance of payments in recent years, nor by

---

[1] A multinational enterprise (MNE) is by definition a direct investor. Herein it is defined as a non-financial company which owns and controls assets in more than one country.

most empirical studies of the determinants of direct investment. To a large degree, many of the difficulties in explaining the determinants of direct investment as a capital flow result from a certain confusion in the treatment of direct investment as a real and as a financial phenomenon.[2] Even where this distinction is made, the previous research in this area, as well as more management-oriented optimization models, has generally assumed a greater degree of perfection in international capital markets than appears to be warranted, at least in the case of capital flows generated by non-financial companies.

By examining the effects of existing market segmentation on the formation of subjective risk perceptions of non-financial investors, the present study seeks to explain the determinants of certain international capital movements associated with the multinational enterprise (MNE), i.e. those flows financing foreign direct investment. It analyses the various ways in which those firms (who have operations abroad and so can be considered multinational) finance their additional foreign-asset acquisitions through the use of three alternative liability flows: home-currency sources, foreign-currency borrowing, and the foreign-generated cash flow of foreign affiliates.

The present study can help to provide clarifications to some issues related to the study of direct investment in three areas: first, from the point of view of capital movement theory, it provides a theoretical basis for explaining important real-world constraints on the otherwise, portfolio-maximizing behaviour of direct investors. Secondly, it provides strong empirical support for the theoretical model and examines the financial behaviour of an important group of multinational enterprises during the transition from fixed to floating exchange-rate regimes (1966–76). Thirdly, the study

---

[2] In much of the previous empirical work, there tends to be a lack of rigour in delineating carefully between balance-sheet relationships so that, often, financial data have been used implicitly to measure changes in the stock of real assets without specifying a behavioural relation between the two. Similar problems arise in specifying the currency denomination of balance-sheet items even in some studies which purport to measure the impact of direct investment flows on the balance of payments.

can shed light on some of the policy concerns in many countries with the balance of payments or resource allocation implications of direct investment flows as capital movements. Most of the previous work has focused on the question of why firms invest abroad, postulating various theories of direct investment. This research, in the main, has considered direct investment from the perspective of real capital transfers (the selection of foreign assets) rather than as financial phenomena (the choice of liabilities). There has been considerable progress in this area of research in recent years.[3] On the other hand, probably in part due to serious data constraints, there has been relatively little research effort devoted to explanations of how these asset acquisitions, which are the basis of the direct investment process, are financed. In the few studies on the financing question,[4] a traditional corporate finance model has normally been employed, distinguishing between internal (to the firm) and external funds or debt and equity to explain how foreign investment is financed. By concentrating instead on the currency denomination of the sources of financing, the present study can be viewed in the context of this economic literature as contributing to an understanding of the balance-of-payments impact of foreign direct investment. It also can be said to advance our understanding of the political economy of MNEs by developing a coherent and simple theory of their financial behaviour.

The theoretical model and empirical results which are presented below do not aspire to develop a new theoretical approach to the question of international capital movements. Rather, it is contended that the assumptions generally made in most of the previous studies on the determinants of international capital movements as applied to direct investment

[3] See, in particular, Raymond Vernon, 'International Investment and International Trade in the Product Cycle', *Quarterly Journal of Economics*, vol. 80, May 1966, pp. 190–207; Richard Caves, 'International Corporations: the Industrial Economics of Foreign Investments', *Economica*, February 1971, pp. 1–27; John Dunning, 'The Determinants of International Production', *Oxford Economic Papers*, November 1973, pp. 289–336; and Peter Buckley and Mark Casson, *The Future of Multinational Enterprise*, London: Macmillan, 1976.
[4] See the survey of the relevant economic and business literature in Chapter IV.

(or to the flows of direct investment from a balance of payments view-point) are mis-specified. This mis-specification stems from simplifying assumptions made concerning the relative perfection of international capital markets. Based upon this theoretical construction, a high degree of capital market integration has been assumed with direct investors acting rationally on full information available in these markets to minimize the cost (or risk) of financing asset acquisitions.

In the present study, these restrictive assumptions are relaxed and the resulting consequences for re-assessing the economic significance of the determinants of the financing decision are then developed and analysed. In other words, while still assuming that direct investors are rational, there may be important real-world constraints on their portfolio maximization behaviour.

The basic premise underlying the hypothesis elaborated below is that direct investors are subject to an 'exchange-rate illusion' in determining the sources of financing their foreign investments.[5] That is, the parent company views foreign-currency assets, at least in the earlier stages of international expansion, as *inherently* riskier in terms of the home-country currency denominated balance sheet and income statement. This is due to the fact that, for a firm maximizing its net worth in home-currency terms, the income stream produced by foreign assets is subject to a random variable, the exchange rate, introducing an extra risk factor for foreign assets and liabilities. The firm's primary reaction is to concentrate on the currency denomination of the components of its consolidated balance sheet. As a consequence, the management of MNE will endeavour to minimize its risk in terms of home currency for financing foreign-currency denominated assets. This behaviour can be seen as being rational on the part of direct investors where the cost to the firm of accept-in the illusion that real wealth is maximized by maximizing home-currency profits will vary with the volatility of exchange

[5] Not to be confused with 'money illusion' in which investors use nominal currency rates, unadjusted for purchasing power equivalents during periods of inflation, in deciding upon asset financing.

rates in terms of home currency. Where this cost is relatively
low, say under a regime of fixed exchange rates, or unper-
ceived, due in part to accounting conventions, then firms will
have little incentive to try to overcome these costs which
would necessitate additional expenditure and management
attention.[6]
This contention holds that international capital market
integration and perfection may not exist nearly to the extent
assumed in an increasingly abundant body of economic literature which maintains that international capital flows are a
stock-adjustment phenomenon resulting from changes in
interest-rate differentials and exchange-rate expectations.[7]
This economic literature ignores the considerable costs to
non-financial companies of overcoming market imperfections.
In this respect, the present study can be viewed as an extension to direct investment as a financial phenomenon of the
'market imperfections' approach which has been successfully
applied to explain direct investment as a real phenomenon
in recent years.[8]
The main hypothesis suggested in this study argues that it
is not the expectations of changes in exchange rates in themselves that primarily determine capital flows, but rather,
for direct investors, the fact that *all* foreign currency denominated assets involve a perceived risk for companies
maximizing their consolidated profits in terms of home-
country currency.
Kindleberger has attributed such behaviour to 'exchange-
rate illusion'.[9] In the present case, this would imply that
companies with foreign operations (MNEs) regard *all* assets
outside the home country, denominated in foreign-currency

6 Under floating exchange rates, the costs of accepting exchange rate illusion
may have risen considerably, so encouraging a learning process for MNEs in which
efforts are made to reduce such costs. This may in turn help to explain the ascend-
ancy of financial managers to the control of many MNEs in recent years compared to the predominant role of marketing managers in the 1960s.
7 See Chapter IV.
8 See the recent survey in A. M. Rugman, 'Internalisation as a General Theory
of Foreign Direct Investment: A Re-appraisal of the Literature', *Weltwirtschaftliches Archiv*, vol. 116, no. 2, 1980.
9 C. P. Kindleburger, *Europe and the Dollar*, Cambridge, Mass.: MIT Press,
1966. Also see pp. 57–8.

terms, as subject to risk, but not those in the home country.

The following theory of the financing of foreign direct investment could be called a theory of risk-reduction in which the 'exchange-rate illusion' is rational on the part of the direct investor who wishes to minimize the risk to the parent company of using home-currency funds to finance foreign assets *even* where interest-rate differentials or exchange-rate expectations would dictate a portfolio shift in favour of such parent-company financing, were such firms to have perfect, costless information available.

The advantage of the present approach is essentially one of greater realism. By focusing on the actual behaviour of an important group of transactors, this study hopes to clarify a contentious issue in the application of recent advances in the theories of capital movements to direct investors. Empirically, not only is an important distinction drawn between direct investment as a real and as a financial phenomenon, but the actual behaviour of a significant group of MNEs in several OECD countries is examined during the transition from fixed to floating exchange rates. The issues involved are significant from a policy point of view as well. Because of their concerns with the impact of direct investment on the balance of payments, many governments, including those of OECD countries, have policies designed to deter or to prevent the financing of foreign direct investment by their residents with home currency.[10] The question arises as to the theoretical and empirical foundations upon which these policies are based.

The present study, while narrowly focused, intends to illuminate some of these issues.

---

[10] See the description of these policies for the countries in the empirical sample in Chapter VII and the OECD report on *International Direct Investment: Policies, Procedures and Practices*, Paris: OECD, 1979.

II METHODOLOGY

The financing of foreign direct investment can be viewed from different perspectives — debt vs. equity, internal funds or external funds, parent-company funds or affiliate funds, and funds denominated in different currencies. The latter distinction in terms of currencies is used here. This stems from a desire to understand direct investment financing as a capital movement phenomenon with balance-of-payments implications.

Capital movements always involve the use of, or the substitution for, foreign exchange. Debt and equity, internal and external sources, and parent and affiliate funds can all be denominated in both home or foreign currencies. Therefore, a differentiation along those lines would not be very useful for understanding the financing of direct investment as a capital flow. The relevant criterion is between home-country currency or foreign currency to finance foreign assets. The question from a balance of payments perspective is: what determines the currency denomination of liabilities with which a company finances its foreign investment?

This question is addressed in what follows below. No attempt is made to carry out an exhaustive treatment of all aspects of the question. To try to explain all factors involved in the determination of the financing process, no matter how insignificant, would be empirically inconclusive, given the present data constraints, and intellectually unproductive due to the complexity of the process in a dynamic context. Rather, the study focuses on the main determinants, attempting to explore the basic causal relationships involved, supported by some empirical evidence. Greater clarity and realism result. Perhaps this methodological approach can best be summed up as follows:

It is easy enough to make models on stated assumptions. The difficulty is to find the assumptions that are relevant to reality. The art is to set up a scheme that simplifies the problem so as to make it manageable without eliminating the essential characteristics of the actual situation on which it is intended to throw light.[1]

With this limited objective in mind, the study seeks to explain the respective roles of net home-currency funds, of foreign-currency borrowing and of the internal cash flow of foreign affiliates in the financing of foreign direct investment. The choice of these variables is explained in Chapter V. The study is divided into three parts:

1. The background and economic significance of the phenomena to be explained, how the relevant economic literature has handled these questions in the past, and the choice of the dependant variables, respectively in Chapters III, IV and V.

2. A theoretical model of risk minimization, consistent with the maximization of the market value of the parent company in its home currency, in order to explain some important capital flows associated with foreign direct investment by multinational enterprise (MNE) — those net home-currency flows financing asset acquisitions abroad, as well as foreign-currency denominated borrowing and cash flow of foreign affiliates, in Chapter VI.

3. An empirical chapter to test the model against aggregate time-series data (sources and uses) for a sample of US direct investors in manufacturing in eight countries from 1966 to 1976, in Chapter VII. The results are assessed and conclusions are drawn in Chapter VIII.

---

[1] Joan Robinson, *Economic Heresies*, London: Macmillan, 1971, p. 141.

III BACKGROUND TO THE DEVELOPMENT OF A THEORY

The Study of Direct Investment as a Financial Phenomenon

This study differs from most previous theoretical work on capital movements which either excludes direct investors in discussing the determinants of capital flows or makes somewhat unrealistic assumptions by implicitly aggregating MNEs with other international financial investors. In studying capital movements as a monetary phenomenon, there has been a tendency to distinguish between short-term and long-term (portfolio and direct investment) transactions. In the portfolio adjustment approach, direct investment was often lumped together with long-term portfolio capital, even though these important economic agents may not behave according to its precepts, at least in the short run. The use of an activity orientation in the past (i.e. focusing on types of transactions rather than the behaviour of economic agents) was often dictated by data constraints as well as by traditional balance of payments concerns with trade and capital flows as an integral part of macro-economic theory.

One of the difficulties encountered with the activity approach has been to find corresponding economic agents who behave accordingly in the real world. These ideas, developed by Leamer and Stern,[1] have led to a search for 'real-world' agents who might behave in ways inconsistent with the predictions for unspecified and unconstrained financial investors operating with objective criteria for perceiving risks.

Non-financial enterprises are primarily concerned with

[1] E. E. Leamer and R. M. Stern, *Quantitative International Economics*, Boston: Allyn and Bacon, 1970.

production and sales, both at home and abroad. In order to carry out this primary function, firms will have to accumulate real assets (plant, property, patents, equipment, inventory, etc.). The portion of this stock located abroad is, of course, what is designated as direct investment. The decisions affecting changes in this stock — the choice of assets underlying the real activity of the firm — are outside the scope of the present study.

The financing of this accumulation may be affected by way of parent-company equity or loans, foreign-currency debt (or equity) or the internal cash flow of each affiliate. Each of these methods will have a direct or indirect impact on international capital transfers.

Financial Flows and the Balance of Payments

As observed in Chapter I, the present study attempts to explain the determinants of the flows which are statistically recorded as 'direct investment' in the balance of payments as well as foreign sources of funds by examining the principal factors governing the foreign asset financing decisions of non-financial companies. The linkage between these two phenomena may not be evident at first glance.

The process of direct investment can be deemed to have two parts. The first is concerned with acquisitions of facilities abroad, i.e. how does a firm decide to service a foreign market (e.g. exporting, licensing, production) and what assets (i.e. fixed assets, inventory, etc.) does it invest in. The second is concerned with the financing of these acquisitions. The first is in the province of industrial economics dealing with the micro-economic analysis of real capital investment and industrial organization. The second is in the scope of international economics dealing with international capital movements.

Most balance-of-payments statistics only record some of the latter financial flows and do not measure real asset accumulation by non-residents. In most countries, only the capital invested in the form of cash by the parent company (equity or loans) is recorded as direct investment. In a few others (Australia, Canada, Germany since 1976, the United Kingdom and the United States) re-invested earnings are also recorded. But all the balance-sheet items necessary to record the acquisition of real assets (local borrowing, funds from affiliates, local equity, depreciation allowances) are not included in even the most complete balance-of-payments statistics.

For instance, how can it be explained that between 1966 and 1976, for a large sample of US-owned foreign affiliates in Europe, only an average of about 7.5 per cent of asset accumulation was financed by a gross outflow of dollars (and that on a net basis, gross outflow less repatriated earnings, the contribution of the US parent companies was negative)?[2] Yet, in the balance of payments, it is the above figure which supposedly measures the flow of direct investment.

In those years, on a balance-sheet basis, almost the entire increase in foreign assets owned by US-controlled companies was financed by the internal cash flow of foreign affiliates (profits plus depreciation allowances) and by funds borrowed from foreign sources, rather than by parent-company contributions of dollar financing (equity or loans). The US controls on outward direct investment did not seem to play a significant role in influencing this financial pattern. The American authorities imposed mandatory ceilings on the dollar financing of foreign direct investment in 1968, which were gradually eased until final removal in 1974. In many cases, the ceilings were not utilized. Even subsequent to the removal of the US controls and where, in addition, interest-rate differentials on a covered basis pointed to parent-company financing, dollar outflows in most cases did not significantly increase. Other bodies of theory, including corporate finance theory (focusing on the cost of capital) or the capital movement literature (explaining flows as portfolio adjustments to interest-rate differentials and exchange-rate expectations) would have predicted much larger outflows from the US. Had that been the case, the balance of

[2] See the discussion of the data in the empirical Chapter VII, especially pp. 100–4.

payments implications for the home and host countries would have been significantly different. An adequate theory should be able to explain this behaviour of such economically significant agents as direct investors (or MNEs).

Capital flows, particularly those of direct investment by multinational enterprises, have become an issue of public policy in many countries. Regulation at the national and international levels of the financial activities of MNEs has been called for in several instances. The OECD has already developed guidelines[3] and the UN is trying to elaborate a code of conduct for multinational enterprises which would include standards relating to their financial policies.

Yet for all the discussion and promulgation of directives, there has been surprisingly little systematic analysis of the determinants of the foreign-financing decision. Heretofore, in most academic and governmental studies, the focus (on the financial side) has been on the methods and procedures (including evasion via transfer pricing or the use of tax havens, etc.) of international money management with all of the potential ramifications for the balance of payments if such circuits were actually to be used. From this policy perspective, the concern has been with the *potential* ability of MNEs to shift large amounts of liquid funds between countries which could severely affect exchange rates and the balance of payments. Some empirical studies have described some of this money movement but without attempting to analyse the determinants of this activity.[4] Even the mandatory US controls applied from 1968 to 1974 appeared to have almost no theoretical underpinnings except for a permanent concern with the potential for capital outflows available to US direct investors.

The present study offers an explanation as to why MNEs have not generally used their potential ability to shift large amounts of liquid funds internationally for non-operational purposes.

Multinational enterprises are generally believed by some

[3] *Declaration on International Investment and Multinational Enterprises*, Paris: OECD, June 1976.
[4] See Chapter IV.

observers of the international economic system to be able to operate across national frontiers and exchange control procedures in order to maximize their profits from a currency fluctuation, or to protect themselves from its consequences. According to this hypothesis, the enormous volumes of foreign exchange that MNEs generate through intra-company payments, either financial or trade-related, are highly manoeuvrable. The object of international money management is to place assets in appreciating currencies and to place debts in currencies likely to depreciate. In this hypothetical approach taught at many graduate business schools[5] it is not always clear whether the agent is a risk-taker or risk-averter, that is whether the goal is the maximization of profits through outright speculation or rather a question of hedging to protect assets and to cover liabilities at the global level which worldwide investments require. The effect of such strategies, if implemented, would be to add to the pressures for the parity changes anticipated, as feared by the governmental authorities concerned.

The present study attempts to elucidate some of the issues referred to above by going beyond casual empiricism to examine a relatively simple yet plausible theory of determinants of financial behaviour of MNEs. An empirical model is accordingly postulated and tested.

Non-financial Investors in a Multiple Currency World

Recalling the two notions of direct investment described above as real and financial phenomena, it is contended that they can be treated separately, depending upon the objective of the analysis. In this sense, the present study is consistent with the approach usually followed in studies of corporate finance. Decisions concerning ways to finance a direct investment are no different in principle from decisions

---

[5] See, for instance, S. H. Robock, K. Simmonds, and J. Zwick, *International Business and Multinational Enterprises*, Homewood, Illinois: Richard D. Irwin, Inc., 1977 revised edition, Chapter 21.

concerning ways to finance a domestic investment.[6] In this approach, in the short run, the asset-investment decision can be taken as given. The decision by the parent company to finance a foreign operation with its home-currency denominated assets or with foreign-currency demoninated funds, whether internal or external to the MNE as a whole, can be studied just as one would study the choice between, say, home and foreign borrowing. It can essentially be described by a model of risk-reduction along the lines of a portfolio optimization model which, while acknowledging the importance of interest rates and exchange risks, incorporates notions of financial and operating risks due to market segmentation ('exchange rate illusion') encountered by international non-financial companies.

One of the major contentions of the model developed below to describe the financing of foreign asset accumulation by direct investors is that currency denomination determines financing preferences based upon risk perceptions, more so than the maturity or cost of debt. Of course, the notion of risk, like that of expectations, involves subjective criteria and therefore is not as amenable to the development of an analytical model as objective criteria such as costs. Nevertheless, a model attempting to explain certain kinds of international financial decisions which excludes such considerations may be, at best, only indicative or, at worst, irrelevant.

The model developed here assumes that the parent company wishes to maximize its perceived wealth in terms of home curency. The key role of the home currency — that in which most of the firm's sales, its shares and its financial statements are denominated — will be developed in Chapter VI below. The wealth maximization assumption as the standard approximation for the actual behavioural motivation of firms would seem to be particularly appropriate for MNEs. As most MNEs are large, quoted companies, they are subject to close scrutiny by brokers, investment bankers and institutional investors. Any significant deviation from the

[6] Kenen, for instance, insists upon the use of the portfolio approach in P. B. Kenen, 'Capital Mobility and Financial Integration: A Survey', *Princeton Studies in International Finance* no. 39, Princeton University, 1976.

maximization of shareholder's wealth would provoke adverse trading in a company's shares and encourage take-over bids or possibilities of changes in management (see pp. 71–2).

The basic working hypothesis in the model is the assumption that there is an identifiable and continuing relationship between different types of foreign-asset holdings and the liabilities in home or foreign currencies to finance these assets. Annual flows (sources and uses) of funds are assumed to be consistent with these relationships. Such an assumption, based upon the balance-sheet identity is the essence of the portfolio approach and one of the main hypotheses underlying corporate finance theory. The novel aspect in the assumption made here is to differentiate between liabilities in various currencies rather than those of various maturities, etc. The basic quality separating preferences for various liabilities remains the same: the differing degree of risk associated with various types of liabilities. Thus, a risk-reduction approach could apply to the choice of debt and equity to finance balance-sheet changes as well as the choice between home and foreign currencies.

This model was chosen in the belief that direct investors tend to finance foreign assets with funds in different currencies so as *to minimize the direct investors' financial exposure to various events over which they have no control.* For one of the fundamental characteristics of the environment for direct investors is the large number of currencies in which the firm is obliged to conduct its operations. The operations of the affiliates are almost always translated into the currency of the home country as a 'numéraire' for consolidation into the corporate accounts for eventual scrutiny by actual and potential shareholders, and for purposes of management control in order to evaluate the home-currency consequences of specific foreign operations.

It might be noted that there are, in fact, two categories of measures which are important in relating possible exchange-rate changes to the parent-company's accounts. There is 'conversion' which describes exchange losses or gains that result when one currency must be changed or 'converted' into another currency in order to settle outstanding liabilities.

All assets abroad, including fixed assets (unless they are fully depleted with no scrap value), are eventually subject to 'conversion' losses or gains. 'Translation' exchange losses or gains occur when a financial statement expressed in one currency is 'translated' so as to be expressed in another currency; in translation, one currency is not actually exchanged for another. Unlike actual or 'conversion' losses or gains, 'translation' methods are governed by accounting conventions or regulations. For instance, the 'current/non-current methods' endorsed by the American Institute of Certified Public Accountants prescribes the translation of long-term assets and equities at historical rates whereas short-term assets and liabilities should be translated at the exchange rate in effect on the date of the balance sheet.

Accounting considerations, to the extent that they impact on the reported earnings of companies, may be of crucial importance in the choice of currencies to finance the acquisition of foreign assets. In the final analysis, it will be the accounting rules in each country that determine what a given company has at 'risk' in foreign currencies. The application of these rules will vary from firm to firm and over time. So a certain degree of caution is warranted when discussing the general effects of accounting rules on the currency exposure of companies. For instance, in 1976, the Financial Accounting Standards Board in the US issued its Statement No. 8, requiring that fixed assets abroad be translated into dollars at the rate in effect when the assets were acquired, known as the 'historical rate'. But current assets, current liabilities and long-term debt must be translated at the exchange rate as of the date of the balance sheet. Any translation losses or gains must be reflected directly in consolidated earnings. As fixed assets are valued at historical rates whereas most liabilities to finance them are valued at current rates, in a period where the dollar is depreciating relative to a host-country currency, foreign-currency borrowing becomes relatively expensive, negatively affects balance-sheet ratios and generates translation losses. FASB No. 8 would encourage the use of dollar financing of foreign fixed assets. Unfortunately, post-1976 data are not available to investigate this issue in the present study. This would be particularly interesting in light of the recent proposed changes to FASB No. 8 which may be effective in December 1981. These changes should, from an accounting point of view, encourage behaviour as shown in this study. One of the most important changes would require US companies to use current exchange rates when translating all foreign operations into dollars. Another important change would require companies to show certain adjustments resulting from translation of foreign-currency statements as part of stockholder's equity, rather than as earnings (conversion gains and losses would continue to be shown as earnings, however).

The business literature has long recognized the importance of financial planning techniques in which affiliates are assigned budget profit targets in terms of the home currency.[7] If the corporate headquarters are in the United States, for example, it is accustomed to operating in US dollars. Furthermore, the dollar is the currency which the headquarters use to report the company's performance to the share-holders (through the corporate income statement and balance sheet). Consequently, budgeted financial statements in US dollars are needed to review the contribution of each foreign affiliate to the worldwide corporate profits. Monitoring the actual performance (actual contribution to corporate profits) of the foreign affiliate also requires financial statements expressed in terms of dollars. For internal control purposes, many multinational enterprises use the 'current exchange rate' method to translate all assets and liabilities at the exchange rate in effect on the date of the balance sheet.

Whatever 'translation' method is used, the MNE is nevertheless confronted with a certain degree of uncertainty concerning the home-currency value of profits earned abroad by foreign affiliates. Besides the 'translation' method used and whether 'conversion' takes place, the home-currency value of a given amount of foreign-currency earnings will depend on two factors: (1) the financial composition of the balance

---

[7] See, for example, E. C. Bursk, J. Dearden, D. F. Hawkins, and U. M. Longstreet, *Financial Control of Multinational Operations*, New York: Financial Executives Research Foundation, 1971, pp. 22, 25.

sheet of each affiliate, and (2) the economic conditions in foreign countries such as inflation and exchange-rate changes. The management of a MNE has obviously no control over the second group of factors, and to the extent that the asset decisions are dictated by operational requirements as argued on pp. 91–2, it can only control the liability side of the affiliate's balance sheet. Even there, numerous constraints limit management's ability to choose its sources of financing (e.g. depreciation is a function of past investment, suppliers' credits depend on the level of inventory purchases, etc.).

Self-Protection Against Exchange Risks

Firms wishing to minimize the risk to, say, dollar profits from changes in exchange rates affecting foreign-currency profits can pursue policies, either explicitly or implicitly, to reduce their exposure. Essentially, MNEs can either engage in hedging operations, for instance, selling foreign currency forward for dollars or they can adjust the currency composition of the affiliate's balance sheet.

Hedging through the use of forward contracts is often recommended in the business literature[8] even though its application to direct investors is very limited. The main problem is that hedging is expensive and, even if the timing of a currency rate change is correct, it only provides one accounting period's protection for foreign assets.[9] The forward market for maturities longer than six months is usually thin in any currency. During a crisis period, when hedging is most desired, the margins can widen appreciably, making the cost

[8] See, for instance, J. F. Weston and B. W. Sorge, *International Managerial Finance*, Homewood, Illinois: Richard D. Irwin, Inc., 1972, Chapter Five.

[9] However, hedged positions can be rolled over periodically to provide long-term protection from currency risks. But the cost of the forward contract is re-negotiated in each period so that, unless a correct assessment of the eventual magnitude and timing of the exchange-rate change has been made, such practices can entail significant costs. Such practices, which may be common for financial institutions, may be adopted increasingly by non-financial MNEs in the period of floating exchange rates as the costs of accepting 'exchange rate illusion' rise relative to the costs of overcoming market segmentations so engendering a learning process described in the theory below.

of forward cover a significant percentage of the value of the assets to be protected. Besides the costs and timing uncertainties in the use of forward contracts, there are also often governmental constraints such as past British requirements that hedging be related to commercial transactions involving the movement of goods, or French limits on the maturities of forward contracts (usually 30 days). Other, somewhat more esoteric, forms of hedging are theoretically available to firms such as forward options, currency swaps, exchange repurchase agreements or extended governmental risk guarantees (in developing countries). These potential methods are often extensively discussed[10] but of little use in practice, due to their cost, level of requisite sophistication and co-ordination, and limited ability to protect 'exposed' assets of on-going concerns.[11] Generally, most hedging techniques seem to warrant a degree of capital-market perfection that does not exist in reality so that many of these methods remain illustrative rather than practical, at least for non-financial firms investing in long-term assets.

Alternatively, MNEs might adjust the currency composition of their affiliates' balance sheets so as to reduce their exposure to currency changes. On the asset side, as noted above and on pp. 92–3, the degree of margin is very limited for non-financial companies. Working capital and liquid assets are necessary to the normal functioning of an enterprise. To try to reduce their levels below those required to meet current liabilities could involve costly difficulties and the risk of default. It is contended that the scope for risk reduction on the asset side of the balance sheet is very small except in exceptional circumstances. It is a well-known proposition that if a firm balances its assets and liabilities in each currency, then its net exposure to currency risk will be zero as any impact on assets is fully offset by an opposite impact on an equal amount of liabilities. Simple decision rules result which dictate that MNEs should borrow in each currency,

[10] See, for instance, D. A. Ricks, *International Dimensions of Corporate Finance*, Englewood Cliffs, N.J.: Prentice-Hall, 1978.

[11] See S. M. Robbins and R. B. Stobaugh, *Money in the Multinational Enterprise*, New York: Basic Books, 1973, pp. 128–31, on the limitations in the use of hedging techniques by MNEs in practice.

depending on relative interest rates and the possibility and extent of currency changes, to finance assets denominated in foreign currency. In effect, the present study is an attempt to elucidate the theoretical basis and empirical consequences of this common-sense management technique. The question for a wealth-maximizing company faced with the uncertain home-currency value of foreign earnings is how to decide upon the currency composition of its balance sheet. This question and an economically plausible response are developed in Chapter VI on a theory of financing of foreign direct investment.

IV   THE SCOPE OF THE PREVIOUS WORK

The approach taken in the present study to analyse the determinants of foreign-asset financing can be seen as a logical
extension of previous work in the field, combining developments in the economic literature of international capital
movements with those of corporate financial theory. A new
theory of international capital movements is not presented.
Rather, what follows from the presentation in this chapter
is a new interpretation of direct investment phenomena
stemming from the mis-specification of some assumptions in
previous explanations of capital flows as applied to the
financing of direct investment. The basic assumption of these
theoretical models that is questioned here is the explicit or
implicit view of a high degree of international capital market
perfection.

   In such models, it is usually postulated that, given an
initial distribution of wealth, no transactions costs, and perfect information, capital flows will be a function of interest
rate differentials (or changes in differentials), i.e. return
criteria, and of differing subjective perceptions of risk including exchange rate expectations, i.e. risk criteria. This market
perfection assumption contributed to the early analysis of
capital flows as independent activities by traders, interest
arbitrageurs and speculators in the forward market. Later,
it was used to develop more comprehensive theories of
portfolio-adjustment to explain both short- and long-term
capital movements.

   As will be discussed in this chapter, there are two major
draw-backs to this approach as applied to capital flows
financing direct investment. One is a methodological confusion between flows of assets and flows of liabilities. In most
capital-movement theory, it has been usually assumed that

the transaction in assets (e.g. bonds, shares, trade credits) is accompanied by a liability flow in the opposite direction such that, when an American investor purchases a British bond (i.e. asset), there is a dollar transfer to finance the transaction (i.e. a liability flow). This assumption might be quite untrue for portfolio investment in some cases (i.e. during the forty some-odd years of UK exchange controls – until 24 October 1979 – the purchase of foreign securities by British investors did not involve any net sterling financing). For direct investment, such an amalgamation between flows of assets (i.e. acquisition of property, plant, equipment, inventory, trademarks, etc.) and flows of liabilities to finance foreign-asset acquisitions (which may involve large proportions of foreign-generated funds and, hence, *no* international financial capital movement) may be plainly misleading. After all, as Dunning[1] has suggested, the real distinctiveness of MNEs lies not so much in the 'foreignness' of their capital, but rather in their other resources, including managerial control. Some theorists have simply ignored this difficulty by postulating that direct investment as a real phenomenon is determined by different perceptions of financial risk by different national investors. Aliber attributes this to currency preferences,[2] while Laffargue emphasizes differing liquidity preferences.[3] Other writers, even very recently, are still confusing direct investment as a real phenomenon that the they wish to explain with data or variables involving changes in liabilities.[4]

The second draw-back is more substantial and relates to the empirical question of whether capital markets are as perfect as assumed in most of the economic theory related to capital movements, at least as far as non-financial investors

[1] J. H. Dunning, 'Multinational Enterprises and Domestic Capital Formation', in J. S. G. Wilson and C. F. Scheffer (eds.), *Multinational Enterprises – Financial and Monetary Aspects*, Leiden: A. W. Sijthoff, 1974, pp. 159–60.

[2] R. Z. Aliber, 'A Theory of Direct Foreign Investment', in C. P. Kindleberger (ed.), *The International Corporation: A Symposium*, Cambridge, Mass: MIT Press, 1970.

[3] J. P. Laffargue, 'Une Explication Economique des Flux d'Investissements Directs entre Pays Hautement Industrialisés', *Revue Economique*, May 1971.

[4] J. Lunn, 'Determinants of United States Direct Investment in the E.E.C.: Further Evidence', *European Economic Review*, January 1980.

are concerned. That is, even with the asset decision as given, are the barriers to capital movements (high transactions costs, poor information, differing views of risk of foreign exchange, government controls) so low that direct investors will always finance their foreign asset acquisitions in the 'cheapest' market? This study is addressed to this latter question. But before developing an explanatory model, it would be useful to review some of the background in the economic literature.

Early Studies of Short-term Capital Movements

Therefore, the study of international capital movements, including direct investment, tends to be fraught with difficulties, most of which stem from the fact that a capital movement is a monetary, not a real phenomenon. The early controversy focused on mechanisms by which real goods corresponding to a given financial flow would be transferred from one nation to another. Ricardo emphasized income mechanisms;[5] Hume[6] and Taussig[7] attributed greater influence to price changes while Viner[8] underlined the importance of the role of diverging price levels. Prior to the collapse of the gold exchange standard, this discussion was situated within the framework of the classical price–specie–flow theory and of the more modern quantity theory of money applied to an open economy. Capital movements in this system were essentially determined by international differences in yield with no distinction made between portfolio and direct investments.

Classical transfer theory rarely distinguished between the various purposes and destinations of capital flows. Meade[9] and Johnson[10] emphasized the links between capital movements

[5] David Ricardo, *On the Principles of Political Economy and Taxation*, 1817.

[6] David Hume, *Essays and Treatises on Several Subjects*, vol. I, 1752.

[7] F. W. Taussig, *International Trade*, New York: Macmillan, 1927.

[8] J. Viner, *Canada's Balance of International Indebtedness, 1900–1913*, Cambridge, Mass.: Harvard University Press, 1924.

[9] J. E. Meade, *The Balance of Payments, the Theory of International Economic Policy*, vol. I, London: Oxford University Press, 1951.

[10] H. G. Johnson, 'The Transfer Problem and Exchange Stability', *Journal of Political Economy*, June 1956.

and national monetary sectors, however, and laid the foundation for a modern theory of balance-of-payments adjustment.

In more recent years, since the European currencies became convertible in 1958 and forward operations began again, efforts have been made to define rigorously the mechanism of financial flows, generally short term, as an integral part of the foreign exchange market and to specify the determinants of such flows. At first, capital movements were studied as a flow phenomenon with the flows related to levels of other variables such as interest-rate differentials.

Such was the theoretical model pioneered by Tsiang[11] which demonstrated how hedging, speculation and interest arbitrage, on the one hand, and supply and demand factors on the spot exchange market on the other, together played a role in determining an equilibrium for both the spot and forward exchange rates. This integration of the spot and forward exchange markets was a key to the explanation of international short-term capital flows. The essential, and rather obvious, point being that it is the existence of different currencies with different actual and expected rates of return that create financial, as opposed to real, capital flows.

Tsiang's separation of the three functions as independent of one another allowed for a very comprehensive analysis of factors influencing the demand and supply schedules of forward and spot exchanges. This distinction by function greatly simplified the theoretical exposition and was not meant to exemplify the behaviour of any particular group of economic agents. In addition, and of particular notice, is the implicit assumption of perfect markets. It is nevertheless useful to review briefly Tsiang's analysis of forces affecting the equilibrium on the forward and spot exchanges as so much of the subsequent theory is based upon his trichotomy.

Tsiang began with the generally classic assumption that there will be a net flow of short-term capital between two countries unless the forward premium (discount) on one of the two currencies is approximately equal to the difference in relevant short-term interest rates between the two countries.

[11] S. C. Tsiang, 'The Theory of Forward Exchange and Effects of Government Intervention on the Forward Exchange Market', *IMF Staff Papers*, April 1959.

The greater the subjective perception of risk and the higher an arbitrageur's past commitments, however, the larger will be the difference between the forward premium and the interest-rate differential needed to induce him to enter into new forward contracts.[12]

The theoretical specification of speculative activity is quite a difficult problem as its explanation relies on a still unresolved theory of expectations. Tsiang had tried to demonstrate that a speculative position on the spot market could be expressed without loss of generality as a combination of an open position on the forward market and a covered interest arbitrage operation, implying that an analysis of speculation could be confined to the forward exchange market alone.

The key variables influencing the behaviour of a speculator in the forward exchange market are the difference between the expected spot rate at some future time and the current forward rate for a contract maturing at that same future date, and the speculator's subjective estimate of risk attached to the realization of his expectations. In addition, the speculator's past forward commitments should be included. The speculator's risk basically reflects exchange-rate risk, but it also takes into account the risk of government intervention and control of capital transactions, although this is never specified except as the variable, r_t.[13]

---

[12] An arbitrageur's net demand for (90 days) forward exchange can be expressed as:

$$D_{at} = F\left\{ [P_t - (I_{ft} - I_{dt})], V_{ft}, V_{dt}, A_{at}, \sum_{i=t-1}^{i=89} D_{ai} \right\}$$

with

$$\frac{\partial F}{\partial V_f}, \quad \frac{\partial F}{\partial A_a} > 0; \quad \frac{\partial F}{\partial [P_t - (I_{ft} - I_{dt})]}, \quad \frac{\partial F}{\partial V_d}, \quad \frac{\partial F}{\partial \Sigma D_a} < 0,$$

where P is the forward premium on the foreign currency. I_f and I_d are foreign and domestic interest rates, V_f and V_d are the arbitrageur's subjective estimate of risk, A_a stands for the arbitrageur's total liquid assets, and the last term is the sum of his past commitments.

[13] A speculator's net demand function for (90 days) forward exchange is then:

The essential difficulty with this approach to speculation is that the demand for forward exchange assumes expectations of future rates as exogenously given. Thus, Tsiang's theoretical analysis of the forward and spot exchange markets is inoperative without a theory which would provide a basis for the formation of exchange-rate expectations. The main problem has been to develop an expectation function which would explain both stabilizing and de-stabilizing speculative behaviour, and explicitly develop a theoretical notion of risk in the specification of the determinants.

Among the attempts to deal with stabilizing speculation, Arndt[14] used a concept of adaptive exchange rate expectations based on Baumol's model of speculative behaviour.[15] Arndt assumed that a speculator's demand for foreign exchange was a function of deviations of the current observed rate from some expected normal rate. This approach leads to the familiar Koyck-type distributed lag model in which the demand for foreign exchange by speculators, resulting in a speculative capital flow, is a function of the change in the exchange rate and of the speculative demand from the preceding period. The coefficient of the latter variable is inversely related to the length of the adjustment period. This theoretical approach to speculative behaviour has acquired considerable usage in recent years.

The major weakness of such an approach to the formation

$$D_{st} = S\left\{(ER_t - FR_t), r_t, A_{st}, \sum_{j=t-1}^{t-89} D_{sj}\right\}$$

with

$$\frac{\partial S}{\partial(ER - FR)}, \quad \frac{\partial S}{\partial A_s} > 0; \quad \frac{\partial S}{\partial r}, \quad \frac{\partial S}{\partial \Sigma D_s} < 0,$$

where ER is the expected foreign exchange rate in 90 days, FR is the 90-day forward rate, r is the speculator's subjective risk in undertaking forward contracts, and A_s stands for his total liquid assets.

[14] S. W. Arndt, 'International Short-Term Capital Movements: A Distributed Lag Model of Speculation in Foreign Exchange', *Econometrica*, January 1968, pp. 59–70.

[15] W. J. Baumol, 'Speculation, Profitability and Stability', *Review of Economics and Statistics*, August 1957, pp. 263–71.

of expectations is that it relies on a past performance of the dependent variable as the only explanatory factor. In speculation on the foreign exchange market, the past performance of the rate itself is bound to be only one among a number of factors in the mind of speculators, who try to predict the future spot rate on the basis of a variety of indicators at hand. Furthermore, a rather rigid, exponentially decreasing path of past influences inherent in the Koyck distributed lag model is another unrealistic feature of this approach when, in fact, the lag is likely to be highly variable.

Attempts to handle de-stabilizing speculative movements have been even more complicated because of the discontinuities which existed under a fixed exchange-rate system as the spot rate approached the band and because of the complexity of motives influencing speculative behaviour under such conditions. Each country, each capital market, and each economic agent in a particular time period has specific features which may be major factors in the formation of risks.

An important proportion of short-term capital movements consists of credit arising from trade transactions contracted for future payments. From a theoretical point of view and assuming perfect capital markets, traders and other non-financial economic agents should obtain finance from the source where interest rates are the lowest. Thus by hedging (i.e., covering forward their trade-credit contracts), traders effectively behave as interest arbitrageurs. In line with his methodology of separating the analysis by activity, Tsiang assumed that all traders hedge. Such an assumption is quite unrealistic, however, given that traders do tend to speculate either through leaving trade-credit contracts uncovered, or through leads and lags.[16]

[16] The individual importer's demand for foreign exchange, D_m, and the individual exporter's supply of foreign exchange, S_x, in the forward market can be expressed as:

$$D_{mt} = N[M'_t, [P_t - (I_{ft} - I_{dt})], V_{ft}, V_{dt}, (ER_t - FR_t), r_t]$$

with

Therefore, it would follow that participation in the forward exchange market by traders as hedger-speculators is determined by the size of their short-term trade contracts and by a mean–variance analysis which would balance possible exchange gains from risky credit transactions not covered forward against the forward cover costs of risk minimization by hedging. It should be observed that this speculation, if it is the form of uncovered credit transactions by traders, differs from the usual activity by speculators on the forward market only in the degree of risk aversion; this, of course, is an important distinction since for traders, operating profits will normally be valued much more than speculative profits on the exchange market. The same point would probably apply even more to MNEs who own foreign currency generating assets abroad.

According to the preceding analysis, the equilibrium on the forward exchange market is achieved at a forward rate at which that market is cleared. At that rate, net arbitrageur's supply of forward foreign exchange is equal to the sum of the demand by speculators and traders.[17] An important contribution of Tsiang's was to clarify the essential role of arbitrageurs in creating the link between the spot and forward markets. The arbitrageurs take the spot rate as an exogenous variable and adjust the forward rate in such a way as to achieve an equilibrium on both spot and forward markets.

$$\frac{\partial N}{\partial M'}, \quad \frac{\partial N}{\partial V_f}, \quad \frac{\partial N}{\partial (ER - FR)}, \quad \frac{\partial N}{\partial r} > 0, \quad \frac{\partial N}{\partial [P - (I_f - I_d)]}, \quad \frac{\partial N}{\partial V_d} < 0,$$

$$S_{xt} = Y[X'_t, [P_t - (I_{ft} - I_{dt})], V_{ft}, V_{dt}, (ER_t - FR_t), r_t]$$

with

$$\frac{\partial Y}{\partial X'}, \quad \frac{\partial Y}{\partial [P - (I_f - I_d)]}, \quad \frac{\partial Y}{\partial V_d}, \quad \frac{\partial Y}{\partial r} > 0; \quad \frac{\partial Y}{\partial V_f}, \quad \frac{\partial Y}{\partial (ER - FR)} < 0,$$

where M' and X' stand for imports and exports financed by short-term capital.

[17] In terms of the preceding three equations in the footnotes, the net demand for forward foreign exchange, NDF_t, is zero.

$$NDF_t = D_{at} - (D_{st} + D_{mt} - S_{xt}) = 0.$$

Therefore, it is demonstrated by the foregoing analysis that in the process of achieving a full equilibrium on the exchange markets, the forward exchange rate is an endogenous variable.

This analysis of the equilibrium conditions in the forward and spot markets was an essential step forward in clarifying the relationship between forces which influence short-term capital movements. It can be seen that the model is, in a number of important respects, a partial equilibrium model. Changes in some of the exogenous variables, such as expected exchange-rate changes and interest-rate differentials, are most important in influencing short-term capital movements. However, these determinants may, themselves, be influenced by the international movement of short-term capital assets.

Building upon Tsiang's analysis, Rhomberg,[18] Bell,[19] Kenen[20] and Stein,[21] concentrated on basically empirical investigations of the sensitivity of financial flows to changes in interest rates and in foreign trade. The major point at issue was whether financial flows in general, and short-term capital movements in particular, are a function of absolute interest differentials or whether they respond to a change in these differentials. That is, one view was that arbitrageurs' activity will generate financial flows whenever the gap between the interest rates exceeds the international differences in risk, while the other view was that capital movements were influenced by a change in the international interest differentials. This would mean that in an equilibrium situation, stocks of domestic capital abroad and of foreign capital at home were determined by the existing interest differentials, while international flows would occur if these differentials were disturbed.

Rhomberg and Kenen used flow models while Bell tested

---

[18] R. R. Rhomberg, 'A Model of the Canadian Economy under Fixed and Fluctuating Exchange Rates', *Journal of Political Economy*, February, 1964.

[19] P. W. Bell, 'Private Capital Movements and the United States Balance of Payments', *Factors Affecting the United States Balance of Payments*, Hearings before the Joint Economic Committee, 87th Congress, 1962.

[20] P. B. Kenen, 'Short-term Capital Movements and the United States Balance of Payments', *Factors Affecting the United States Balance of Payments*, Hearings before the Joint Economic Committee, 87th Congress, July 1963.

[21] J. L. Stein, 'International Short-term Capital Movements', *American Economic Review*, March 1965.

a stock model. In all three studies the models were tested on an *ad hoc* basis as no theoretical reasons were provided. Bell found little evidence that movements of short-term US claims on, or liabilities to, foreigners, or their components were very sensitive to changes in international interest-rate differentials. Kenen, on the other hand, who found a significant relationship applied a quadratic form of the expected utility function, as had been done by Tobin[22] and Markowitz,[23] in order to formalize the profit-maximizing behaviour of risk-averse traders who are arbitrageurs, hedgers and speculators at the same time. Cohen[24] analysed further the interest sensitivity of capital movements by incorporating and extending the respective stock and flow models of Bell and Kenen. Branson's use of the portfolio selection theory, based on a mean of expected returns and on the variance of their subjective distribution enabled him to obtain a more specific formulation of speculative behaviour. It was observed by Feldstein,[25] however, that the portfolio selection analysis can generate determinate results only under rather restrictive assumptions.

One of the advantages of using portfolio selection theory in the analysis of capital movements is that such a theory can explain cross hauling (i.e., simultaneous two-way international capital flows between two countries). A demand for foreign assets is viewed as a component of the total assets demand function by a given region of asset holders under conditions of risk. The supply is determined within a framework of the total assets demand function by asset holders abroad. A theoretical basis was thus provided for the separate estimation of foreign assets and foreign liabilities of a given country since these are determined by different functions.

Over a certain period of time, a rearrangement of investors'

[22] J. E. Tobin, 'Liquidity Preference as Behaviour Towards Risk', *Review of Economic Studies*, February 1958.

[23] H. M. Markowitz, 'Portfolio Selection', *Journal of Finance*, March 1952.

[24] B. J. Cohen, 'A Survey of Capital Movements and Findings Regarding their Interest Sensitivity', *Factors Affecting the United States Balance of Payments*, Hearings before the Joint Economic Committee, 87th Congress, July 1963.

[25] M. S. Feldstein, 'Mean-variance Analysis in the Theory of Liquidity Preference and Portfolio Selection', *Review of Economic Studies*, January 1969.

portfolios occurs in response to changes in exogenous variables. When aggregated, this leads to an adjustment in stocks of assets among the two or more countries which will also be completed, ceteris paribus, over a period of time. Thus, a portfolio selection theory provides an explanation of adjustments in stocks in the form of a distributed lag model. Hendershott[26] and Leamer and Stern[27] have observed that considerable difficulties may arise in trying to distinguish a stock adjustment from a flow process if the adjustment is spread evenly over a large number of periods.

Another important aspect of the portfolio selection theory as applied to international capital movements, observed by Floyd[28] and Willett and Foret,[29] consists in the role played by a comparative growth of total assets as determinants influencing asset reallocation among countries. Thus, even if the interest-rate differentials among a set of countries remains constant, capital flows can be thought of as being induced by differences in wealth effects. Not only will a change in the interest rate in one of the countries generate a reallocation of the stock of assets in the portfolios of each country's investors, but it will also cause a change in the continuous flows induced by a comparative wealth effect. Thus, a change in the interest-rate differential among growing economies generates a stock-adjustment effect and a flow-adjustment effect on capital movements, the stock-adjustment induced movements arising from changes in portfolio composition while the flow adjustment induced movements arising when the size of the total portfolio changes. While the former effect is temporary and, ceteris paribus, is completed after a time period, the latter effect causes a smaller, but more sustained, adjustment in the flow of capital.

An analysis of international capital movements within the framework of the growing economy has been made possible

[26] P. H. Hendershott, 'International Short-term Capital Movements: Comment IV', *American Economic Review*, June 1967.

[27] Leamer and Stern, 1970, op. cit.

[28] J. E. Floyd, 'International Capital Movements and Monetary Equilibrium', *American Economic Review*, September 1969.

[29] T. D. Willett and F. Foret, 'Interest-rate Policy and External Balance', *Quarterly Journal of Economics*, May 1969.

by the application of the portfolio selection theory. Also, asset diversification in the same context can successfully explain simultaneous cross flows of assets and liabilities among countries.

Despite these relative advances in capital movement theory, there are also serious weaknesses in this approach as a basis for developing a robust theory of financial capital flows. While some weaknesses are inherent in the portfolio selection theory itself, others result from its application to the process of international short-term capital movements.

The basic portfolio adjustment model − with the proportion of foreign assets in a given stock of wealth as a function of interest-rate differentials, a measure of risk and the wealth variable − has been used to explain individual items on the capital account as well as the net magnitude of capital flows. The inadequacies of this kind of model have been revealed in recent studies and surveys: these criticisms will be reiterated and commented upon to demonstrate the difficulties of treating capital flows in general, much less those financing direct investment.

In order to correctly assess these shortcomings, it might be helpful to outline the basic stock-adjustment model as developed by Branson[30] which has been incorporated into most recent studies of short-term capital movements. Branson used the Markowitz-Tobin model of portfolio selection to explain the allocation of wealth between domestic and foreign assets. Thus, the proportion of foreign assets (B^f) in a given stock of wealth (W) is a function of the domestic and foreign interest rates (R and R'), a measure of risk (E), and the stock of wealth:

$$B^f/W = f(R, R', E, W)$$

An equation explaining capital flows is obtained by taking first differences on both sides of the equation. This yields,

$$\Delta B^f = f(R, R', E, W)\Delta W + f_R W \Delta R + f_{R'} \cdot W \Delta R'$$
$$+ f_E W \Delta E + f_W W \Delta W + u$$

[30] W. H. Branson, *Financial Capital Flows in the United States Balance of Payments*, Amsterdam: North Holland, 1968.

where u is the error term. The first component of the right side measures the continuing flow effect of portfolio growth on capital flows, while the second part measures the stock effect of portfolio adjustment associated with changes in interest rates and other relevant variables. Most authors have ignored the flow effect and instead use a linear form of the above equation,

$$\Delta B^f = a_0 + a_1 \Delta R + a_2 \Delta R' + a_3 \Delta E + u.$$

This basic form – with a variety of explanatory variables – has been used to explain individual items on the capital account as well as the net magnitude of capital flows.

The first point is the well-known problem of simultaneous-equations bias which arises when the domestic interest rate is affected by capital flows. There are various simultaneities between assets and between countries plus supply and demand conditions in each asset/country cell. There are also problems of aggregating heterogeneous groups of economic agents. It has been shown that the bias of an OLS estimate of the interest sensitivity of capital flows is an increasing function of the 'true' interest sensitivity of capital flows. Therefore, empirical results will tend to seriously under-estimate the interest sensitivity of capital movements.

The second point is that portfolio selection theory, as developed by Tobin, endeavoured to explain the behaviour of a risk-averse investor by a diversification of his assets with respect to a degree of their liquidity. Given the nature of risk, it is reasonable to assume that an investor, operating on an international level, will also minimize risk through geographical diversification. As pointed out by Rhomberg,[31] however, an application of the portfolio selection theory limited to only one end of the maturity structure (i.e., short-term, liquid assets) violates the basic proposition of the theory: more on this point follows on p. 38. What is relevant is not a portfolio shift between domestic and foreign assets so much as between bonds, money and other assets.

A third point is that Markowitz-Tobin's theory is concerned

[31] R. R. Rhomberg, 'Canada's Foreign Exchange Market: A Quarterly Model', *IMF Staff Papers*, April 1960.

with individual financial behaviour whereas the attempt to define a collective utility function to explain the aggregative portfolio selection of institutional investors may prove extremely difficult. Baret[32] has observed that the portfolio behaviour of a proprietor who is investing his own funds is difficult to determine since characteristics other than a possible monetary return enter into his utility function. Much the same could be said for an MNE. In such cases, a two-parametric, mean-variance analysis is clearly inadequate. All these difficulties are particularly relevant when international capital movements are concerned since the portfolio behaviour of a non-financial company is typically that of a proprietor. Thus, a portfolio selection approach based on aggregative behaviour, or on behaviour separated by activities without regard to the nature of transactors, is not sufficiently defined in terms of a two-parametric, mean-variance approach. Leamer and Stern[33] advanced the proposition that portfolio selection analysis based on a somewhat more homogeneous transactor group would be more satisfactory. There are several other difficulties with models based on the portfolio selection theory; one being that the dynamics of capital movements are not adequately handled. The model implicitly assumes that a growth rate of assets is independent of the level and the change in interest rates. In addition, in most of these models, domestic interest rates were viewed as entirely exogenous, which implies that, while the domestic interest rate was allowed to influence capital movements, capital movements themselves did not influence interest rates. An implicit assumption was that monetary authorities adopt sterilization policies so as to counteract the effect of balance-of-payments developments on the domestic money supply or interest rates. Porter[34] has argued that observed interest-rate differentials become more important in explaining capital flows as capital market integration proceeds, but at the same time they become less efficient as a monetary

[32] J. Baret, 'Record of Discussion', in K. Borch and J. Mossin (eds.), *Risk and Uncertainty*, New York: Macmillan, 1968, pp. 117–18.

[33] Leamer and Stern, 1970, op. cit.

[34] M. G. Porter, 'Capital Flows as an Offset to Monetary Policy: the German Case', *IMF Staff Papers*, July 1972.

instrument. A domestic excess demand for money can always circumvent domestic capital markets by borrowing from abroad if there are no controls.

Finally, as observed on p. 22, most of the theoretical work on portfolio flows has assumed implicitly that the adjustment of assets is perfectly offset by corresponding liability flows. But it is possible that transfers of liabilities will not correspond directly to the currency denomination nor the maturity of transactions in assets. Hence, for instance, British portfolio investors could use short-term Eurodollar borrowing to finance purchases of long-term, DM-denominated bonds. A clearer delineation between asset choice and the flows of liabilities to finance these portfolio changes would be warranted. The sheer complexity of introducing certain market imperfections, such as substantial differences in borrowers and lenders rates on given liabilities, has made progress in this area very limited.

Despite these shortcomings, these recent applications of stock-adjustment models represent a significant step forward in the development of a theory of international capital movements, although they are still far from explaining those flows associated with MNEs.

Incorporation of Portfolio Adjustment into Macro-economic Models

An important development was to incorporate financial flows into a more complete macro-economic model of the open economy. An early model by Polak[35] used a quantity theory framework where capital flows were treated as entirely exogenous but the money supply allowed to respond to the balance of payments. His model examined the relationship between changes in the credit creation of the banking system and the balance of payments; a capital movement having an impact on the domestic money supply which in turn influences both income and imports until a balance of

[35] J. J. Polak, 'Monetary Analysis of Income Formation and Payments Problems', *IMF Staff Papers*, November 1957.

payments equilibrium is restored.

Later models based on a Keynesian open-economy basis were used in the analysis of macro-economic policies oriented towards maintaining domestic full employment and equilibrium in the balance of payments simultaneously. International capital movements played an important role in this analysis because the degree of a country's interest sensitivity of capital flows was one of the key elements in determining a feasible policy mix for the internal–external balance as in Mundell.[36]

Other models sought to explain long-term capital movements, including direct investment, involving the transfer of real assets where the current and capital accounts of the balance of payments must be consistent with each other. Borts[37] developed a model of trade and investment flows as real phenomena related to the respective savings and investment functions in trading countries. Feder and Regev[38] sought to give a determinant solution to optimal foreign lending and foreign direct investment by introducing default and expropriation risks into national income models where otherwise foreign and domestic capital are perfect substitutes. Particularly applied to direct investment, however, these two studies assume (the latter one explicitly) that the transfer of real assets corresponds directly to financial capital flows.

A further development consisted in the use of a portfolio balance approach within a macro-economic framework. It basically meant adding to the usual Keynesian open-economy model an additional behavioural equation defining the equilibrium in the asset market and including wealth as an explanatory variable in the expenditure, money and asset demand functions. The portfolio approach permitted a treatment of capital flows as a stock-adjustment phenomenon in the model.

[36] R. A. Mundell, 'The Monetary Dynamics of International Adjustment under Fixed and Flexible Exchange Rates', *Quarterly Journal of Economics*, May 1960.

[37] G. H. Borts, 'Long-Run Capital Movements', in J. H. Dunning (ed.), *Economic Analysis and the Multinational Enterprise*, London: George Allen and Unwin, 1974.

[38] G. Feder and U. Regev, 'International Loans, Direct Foreign Investment, and Optimal Capital Accumulation', *The Economic Record*, September 1975.

Such is the model developed by Kouri and Porter.[39] It is assumed that changes in income, prices and the stock of wealth are exogenously given, along with the associated current account of the balance of payments. Thus, a distinctive feature of this model is that it endogenizes the money supply but, on the other hand, treats the real sector as exogenous to the model. Changes in real variables and changes in the domestic components of the monetary base cause portfolio substitutions which lead both to capital flows and changes in the domestic interest rate. In particular, the capital flow equation that they obtain enables them to estimate directly the effect of changes in domestic monetary policy on capital movements, under the assumption that the monetary authorities do not sterilize the effects of payments imbalances.

The macro-economic portfolio balance approach has been a significant contribution to the development of capital movement theory. There are, however, several shortcomings involved, one of which is that the country in question must be too small to have an effect on the asset position of the rest of the world. Secondly, there is an almost total disregard for capital flows arising from expectations of movements in the exchange rate. On *a priori* grounds, one would think such expectations to be a key determinant. Thirdly, it is difficult to find economic agents at the micro-economic level whose behaviour would conform to that prescribed in the model.

Problems in the Application of Portfolio-adjustment Models

A useful starting point for integrating the micro-economic behaviour of financial flows of MNEs with the macro-economic portfolio balance approach is Johnson[40] in which he discussed the determinants of the mobility of capital. He

[39] P. J. K. Kouri and M. G. Porter, 'International Capital Flows and Portfolio Equilibrium', *Journal of Political Economy*, June 1974.

[40] H. G. Johnson, 'Some Aspects of the Theory of Economic Policy in a World of Capital Mobility', in T. Bagiotti (ed.), *Essays in Honour of Marco Fanno*, Padua: Cedam, 1966.

questioned the view that interest rates are the only significant factor influencing international capital movements, an
assumption that would lump all these flows together into
the class of portfolio investment, ignoring the important
categories of equity and direct investment, which are likely
to be governed more by profit prospects associated with the
level of income than by the interest rates available on financial claims. Thus, a distinction was made between two types
of mobility of capital — mobility in response to changes in
income and the associated changes in the profitability of real
investment (income mobility) and the mobility in response
to changes in relative interest rates (interest mobility).

Johnson provided a useful starting point for a re-examination of the major determinants of capital flows, but the main
stimulus for a dissatisfaction with the present body of literature is provided by Leamer and Stern.[41] They emphasize that
a shift from an activity orientation to a transactor orientation
may yield better results and better economics.

Most existing models of international capital transactions
are based upon a set of independent activities grouped
together in the capital account of the balance of payments
and broken down into short-term (trade, interest arbitrage,
forward market speculation) and long-term (portfolio and
direct investment). Most of the models which have been cited
referred to short-term assets which were thought to respond
primarily to interest-rate differentials and risk variables.
The most recent portfolio-adjustment models have resolved
many difficulties such as the stock vs. flow debate and yet
this approach has important draw-backs; one stems from the
static conception of portfolio adjustment, in which net worth
is taken as given. Capital flows may be more the result of
decisions that influence net worth than of the allocation of
net worth among potential assets.

The greatest shortcoming of the portfolio-adjustment
models must surely be that there are some important economic

[41] E. E. Leamer and R. M. Stern, 'Problems in the Theory and Empirical
Estimation of International Capital Movements', in F. Machlup, W. S. Salant,
and L. Tarshis (eds.), *International Mobility and Movement of Capital*, NBER,
New York: Columbia University Press, 1972.

transactors that do not behave, at least in the short-run, according to their stipulations. One difficulty with activity models, therefore, is that they lead one to believe that corresponding to each activity there exists an identifiable transactor behaving in a specified way. Unfortunately, in the international economy, transactors cannot be identified strictly on the basis of such activities as commercial trade, arbitrage, speculation and long-term investment. Another difficulty with activity models is the lack of independence of the various activities being undertaken. For analytical purposes, it seems logically superior to begin by making the transactor the focus of the analysis, and then proceeding to analyse their activities. One such class of transactors would be MNEs.

Multinational non-financial enterprise is primarily concerned with production and sales, both at home and abroad. In order to carry out this primary function, firms will invest in various assets at home and abroad. The financing of these assets can give rise to capital flows.

Given the complexity of the firm's decisions in the administration of its assets and their financing, and the fact that there are important constraints upon firm behaviour in the short run, it is difficult to see how portfolio adjustment can be more than a distant objective. In the first place, portfolio adjustment tends to ignore all of the short-run financial constraints upon the firm's behaviour. Secondly, it can easily lead to a definition of returns that neglects the complex inter-relationships in the decision-making of firms.

Thus, contrary to the typical portfolio balance, macroeconomic view, there is significant variation in asset and liability preferences among various transactors. One would hardly expect MNEs, commercial banks and official institutions to have the same quadratic utility functions and similar risk perceptions. This means that it will be extremely difficult to construct a single comprehensive model of the capital account that would be capable of encompassing all of the pertinent structural characteristics of the different transactors. When an individual transactor such as an MNE engages in several activities spanning the balance-of-payments accounts, the implicit interdependent decision-making will require a joint analysis comprising the various activities of the transactor.

For the portfolio-balance approach to be valid in analysing the MNE, one would have to assume that these firms are essentially financial institutions with large amounts of un-committed financial assets to invest as a portfolio. This view, however, does not correspond to reality. The flow of resources in any company is primarily devoted to the operational functions of production, sales and investment in which the company is engaged, and unattached financial assets are not a normal feature of these companies. Thus, the assets of a non-financial company are basically committed to current operations. As noted in Chapter I, there has been considerable progress in the literature in recent years on the determinants of direct investment. Much of this literature espouses a 'market imperfections' approach in explaining why firms invest in real assets in various foreign locations and would appear to confirm the view that these assets are not available for financial investment. If this were not the case, one would expect to see non-financial MNEs engaged in all kinds of lending and placement activity normally associated with banks. As Hymer[42] had noted, however, even in developing countries where capital is scarce and expensive, one seldom finds foreign affiliates expanding into diverse and unrelated lines. With assets of direct investors not freely available, capital flows associated with the financing of these assets will require a different kind of analysis incorporating some aspects of a basic portfolio-balance model with significant imperfections in financial markets due to perceptions of risk and other constraints.

Two interesting, but opposing, articles by Heckerman[43] and Aliber[44] respectively do apply exchange risks to direct investment in a portfolio investment tradition. Heckerman

[42] S. H. Hymer, *The International Operations of National Firms: A Study of Direct Foreign Investment*, Ph.D., MIT, 1960, subsequently published by the MIT Press in 1976, Chapter Five.

[43] D. G. Heckerman, 'Exchange Rate Systems and the Efficient Allocation of Risk', *Proceedings of a Symposium on Trade, Growth and Balance of Payments*, University of Chicago, December 1970.

[44] Aliber, in Kindleberger (ed.), 1970, op. cit.

argues that exchange risks do not reduce investment flows because a rational investor maximizes the value of his portfolio not in terms of money, but in terms of real goods and services, i.e. money values deflated by relevant price indices. To maximize only money values, even after taking into account the risk of exchange-rate changes on foreign assets, is to suffer from money illusion (see p. 58 below). An investor therefore will make estimates of the prices of securities in various currencies, the likely course of exchange rates and the expected course of general prices. It is especially important for the investor to estimate the outlook for his own currency, and for the course of domestic prices, since myopia and money illusion are most probable here. A utility-maximizing consumer–investor is not content to invest in his own currency to eliminate exchange risk, since he cannot at the same time eliminate the risk that the domestic price level will rise more than price levels in other countries. In the absence of money illusion, exchange risk must be compared with relative prospective price changes and it cannot be assumed that the value of a portfolio in domestic securities is maximized.

Heckerman equates rationality with perfect information in the formation of expectations regarding risk. His argument counters the theory of direct investment put forward by Aliber in which exchange risk is the key determinant. In Aliber's model, investors consider one currency at a time as the strongest world currency, and are willing to pay premia for securities – equities as well as debt – denominated in that currency. Firms which issue securities in the dominant currency have an advantage over corporations with securities denominated in other currencies, in that their securities command higher prices, and they can issue them more cheaply than can firms issuing securities in other currencies. The former can therefore buy up real assets abroad at higher prices than local companies which issue securities and debt in local currency.

Aliber's theory, heavily criticized for ignoring cross-haul investments and green-field investments as opposed to take-overs, assumes, in contrast to Heckerman, a high degree of capital-market segmentation. In a similar vein, Agmon and Lessard have adopted an approach which incorporates significant market imperfections in the form of barriers to international flows of portfolio capital.[45] They argue that these barriers provide the MNE with a financial advantage over single-country firms.

Application of Corporate Finance Theory to Portfolio Adjustment

Given the limitations on the insights gained from aggregating capital flows financing direct investment with portfolio-adjustment models on the capital balance as a whole and, in particular, the lack of theoretical underpinnings for such aggregations, attention has been increasingly turned to the use of portfolio allocation concepts in conjunction with corporate finance theory. Corporate finance theory stipulates that a profit-maximizing firm, given its investment and dividend decisions, will try to minimize its cost of capital to finance these decisions. Several studies have focused on the application of corporate financial precepts to direct investors within the context of a portfolio optimization approach. Perhaps the most promising of these studies and the one most closely linked methodologically to the present study is an article by Guy Stevens written in 1972.[46] From the point of view of the circumscribed objective pursued here, Stevens' approach suffers from a general bias in the corporate finance approach to portfolio optimization by concentrating mainly on the asset-choice decisions. Stevens investigates which foreign assets are purchased by a direct investor and in what proportions, rather than the financing question itself.

This focus on the asset side of the balance sheet stems from the heritage of the Modigliani–Miller propositions,[47]

[45] Tamir Agmon and Donald Lessard, 'Investor Recognition of Corporate International Diversification', *Journal of Finance*, Sept. 1977.

[46] Guy V. G. Stevens, 'Capital Mobility and the International Firm', in Machlup, Salant, and Tarshis (eds.), op. cit.

[47] Franco Modigliani and M. H. Miller, 'The Cost of Capital, Corporation Finance and the Theory of Investment', *American Economic Review*, June 1958.

according to which the market value of any firm is independent of its capital structure, or put another way, the average cost of capital to any firm is completely independent of its capital structure. If valid, then the choice between domestic and foreign sources of funds to finance foreign-asset accumulation is irrelevant.

The first of the Modligiani–Miller propositions, however, depends upon the assumption that rational investors offset, through self-created leverage, the effects of corporate leverage on the market price of equities in perfect markets. Stevens relies on this thesis to justify his approach that it does not matter how the firm divides the financing of its foreign operations between capital flows from the home country and foreign sources.

But, as Robbins and Stobaugh observe in discussing the Stevens' article, there is no unanimity with respect to the validity of the Modligiani–Miller proposition,[48] while in the international area its application appears to be less relevant. The assumptions are highly restrictive.[49] The 'rationality' of investors is based on objective criteria which are correctly perceived by all actual and potential investors. The subjective evaluation by investors of risk due to the currency denominations of their balance sheets would not be incorporated into this framework. Nor is full information available to investors. Where MNEs do not consolidate their balance sheets, foreign borrowing which is not guaranteed by the parent company may not be considered by investors as adding to the leverage of the enterprise. Moreover, the assumption of perfect markets is ambitious, even when applied to the confines of a single country; in an international context, such an assumption appears highly implausible.[50] Even between such large and well-developed capital markets as New York and London, fully covered interest-rate differentials can sometimes exceed

[48] S. M. Robbins and R. B. Stobaugh, 'Comments' in Machlup, Salant, and Tarshis (eds.), op. cit., pp. 354–65.

[49] See Joseph Stiglitz, 'A Re-examination of the Modigliani–Miller Theorem', *American Economic Review*, December 1969.

[50] For a discussion of the reasons for this lack of perfect equilibrium, see Raymond Vernon, *Manager in the International Economy*, Englewood Cliffs, New Jersey: Prentice-Hall, 1968.

1 per cent — and these represent two major money markets with excellent communications links.[51]

Instead of rejecting the Modigliani–Miller theorem by rejecting one or more of the assumptions on which it is based (identical supply curves of finance for investors and firms; no transactions costs or bankruptcy costs; no interest deductions for the purpose of company taxation,[52] and so on), Stevens accepts their proposition, but uses the extra degrees of freedom presented by financial indeterminacy to impose an additional goal on the firm, so leading to financial determinacy. Stevens postulates the minimization of losses due to exchange-rate fluctuations. This choice of theoretical construct is not defended and the empirical results may be consistent both with a constrained Modigliani–Miller assumption or its rejection in favour of the maximization of the present value of the firm with a given amount and distribution of assets in the short run.

In the light of these considerations, it becomes important for the MNE to select the appropriate policy for the liability side as well as the asset side of its affiliates' balance sheets.

The objective of Stevens' study is to analyse the balance-of-payments impact of financial decisions of US-based direct investors in light of the government regulations to control dollar outflows for such purposes.[53] A model is constructed to explain two real and two financial capital flows associated with the MNE: spending for plant and equipment abroad; the change in current assets held abroad; the flow of direct investment (i.e. additional parent-company capital contribution and reinvested earnings); and the flow of funds raised abroad by foreign affiliates. Equations for the financial flows were derived from a theory of minimization of devaluation risk, subsidiary to, and consistent with, the maximization of

---

[51] Calculated at annual rates from *Main Economic Indicators*, OECD Historical Series, various issues.

[52] This assumption was later qualified in F. Modigliani and M. H. Miller, 'Corporate Income Taxes and the Cost of Capital: A Correction', *American Economic Review*, June 1963.

[53] The Foreign Direct Investment Program (FDIP) was applied voluntarily from 1965 to 1967, and made mandatory in 1968. It was gradually phased out and terminated in 1974.

the market value of the firm. In this formulation, the financial flows are functions of changes in total assets and changes in profits (both of each affiliate).

Stevens' postulation of real-asset flow equations was developed because of his objective to investigate the effect of the US balance-of-payments restraint programme on real and financial changes in direct investment. As the former consideration is not directly related to the present study, our attention can be focused on his approach to the financial equations.

Stevens sets out to explain the determinants of two sources for financing foreign assets of an international firm, i.e. the flow of direct investment being the change in the ownership position of the parent company in foreign affiliates (ΔV) and borrowing abroad by foreign affiliates (ΔF). These two sources are incorporated in a sources and uses (balance-sheet changes) identity, which yields

$$\sum_i \Delta A_i = \sum_i (\Delta V_i + \Delta F_i + u_i) \qquad \text{(i)}$$

where the value of asset accumulations (ΔA), summed over affiliates $i = 0, \ldots, n$, equals the sum of the changes in liabilities and net worth owed to the parent company (ΔV), and the sum of the changes in liabilities and net worth owed to foreigners (ΔF), as well as a random residual flow of liabilities (u_i), assumed to be small.

It is noted that the flow of direct investment (ΔV) can be broken down into its component parts, i.e. net capital outflow from the parent company (NKO) and the parent-company share of retained earnings of foreign affiliates (RE) which is the difference between the affiliate's earnings (E) and repatriated dividends (DIV). Stevens, however, does not develop his model in terms of the disaggregation.

Using the variance of its worldwide profits as the measure of risk, a formal model is presented and a decision rule is derived for the optimal value of borrowings in a given foreign currency. The hypothesis is that the firm tries to minimize this variance subject to its balance-sheet constraints.

Defining worldwide profits as operating profits plus capital gains and, after manipulating this identity to get it expressed in terms of balance-sheet changes, Stevens derives a decision rule from the first order conditions where the firm borrows in each currency up to the point where foreign borrowings are equal to the sum of net profits (after interest payments) earned in the foreign currency (GP_i) and the value of capital denominated in that currency (qK_i),

$$D_i = \frac{GP_i}{1 + r_i} + \frac{qK_i}{1 + r_i} \tag{ii}$$

where D_i is borrowings in a foreign currency and r_i is the interest rate in market i.

Given the rapid adjustment of actual borrowings to the equilibrium levels, it is stated that the flow of foreign-currency borrowings would be functions of changes in the level of foreign currency denominated assets and profits.

The theoretical implications of this relationship can be questioned on several grounds. First, the decision rule which is formulated includes varying parameters if GP_i and qK_i are the independent variables as r_i is also an independent variable. Hence, the first difference as

$$\Delta D_i = \frac{1}{1 + r_i}(\Delta GP_i + \Delta qK_i) \tag{iii}$$

is not correct. It is likely that Stevens noted this fact as, in his empirical tests, he drops all reference to the r_i and tests foreign borrowing only as a function of asset and profit changes. Of a more minor nature, Stevens does not include the exchange rate in his equations although it is the variance of the home-currency value of worldwide profits which is being minimized.

Of somewhat greater concern is a certain confusion in the choice of capital flows to be considered. At several points, Stevens reiterates that he wishes to explain the choice between home and foreign financing of foreign-asset acquisitions, these being synonymous with home and foreign currencies. However, this is not what his variables, ΔF and ΔV represent. While ΔF is in terms of foreign currency, ΔV includes both *NKO*, net capital outflow, and *DIV*, repatriated dividends, which are in terms of home currency and *E*, foreign earnings, which are in terms of foreign currency.

Logically, to express capital flows in terms of currency denominations, Stevens should have separated out the net contribution to foreign-asset financing in home currency, $NKO - DIV$, and locally generated sources of funds *internal to the affiliates*, i.e. E, earnings, plus depreciation allowances. It might be noted that Stevens does not even refer to depreciation as a source of asset financing even though asset replacement is its very function and it tends to be the largest single source for financing foreign assets.

On the empirical side, Stevens does not test the formal model which he postulated. Instead he tests foreign borrowing as a function of asset and profit changes, or

$$\Delta F = \alpha \Delta A + \Delta E \qquad \text{(iv)}$$

where α is the percentage of total asset changes denominated in foreign currencies. Upon testing this model and finding the role of earnings changes rejected (*t*-ratio of 0.54 with the wrong sign), Stevens drops the earnings variable in his further tests. The explanatory value of the theory of exchange-loss minimization is significantly reduced by excluding profits. There seems to be no economically justifiable reason for doing so. Otherwise, foreign borrowing is positively related to changes in total assets without regard to profits. It is difficult to see how possible exchange losses could be minimized in such a situation unless, (1) other techniques are used to protect the home-currency value of profits denominated in foreign currencies, such as the use of forward market operations, or (2) the change in total assets already incorporates the effect measured by the use of the change in earnings. If, for example, earnings are accumulated in the affiliate and held in liquid balances abroad until the beginning of the new year before being transferred to the home country, the value of the change in total assets, measured as it is at year-end, would already incorporate the change in earnings.

One of the major contributions of the Stevens' study is to distinguish clearly between the decisions to invest in foreign assets (the direct investment decision) and the choice of liabilities to finance these assets. This distinction has the advantage of approximating the real-world behaviour of non-financial firms in which the function of financial management is to secure financing at minimum cost of the assets chosen by the operational requirements of the firm. From a theoretical point of view, it avoids the ambiguity of those models which confuse the determinants of direct investment as real and financial phenomena.

The fundamental weakness of the Stevens' analysis shared with other studies referred to below, is the choice of liabilities whose determinants are examined. Stevens sets out to explain the balance-of-payments impact of capital flows financing asset accumulation abroad by direct investors. Two sources of financing are distinguished: foreign borrowing by affiliates and direct investment flows from the parent company. By not distinguishing between the net parent-company contribution and reinvested earnings, the currency denomination of the financial sources cannot be distinguished so that the balance-of-payments impact cannot be isolated. An earlier Department of Commerce empirical model had made this distinction.[54]

On the other hand, this is not to contend that the internal cash flow of an affiliate be equated, in a formal sense with other sources of foreign-currency financing, although, from a legal point of view, these funds belong to the foreign affiliate, not to the parent company. Strictly speaking, internal cash flow is only denominated in foreign currency as a numéraire. Theoretically, the parent company can always repatriate 100 per cent of its foreign earnings. As contended in the theory set out below, however, direct investors do regard the internal sources of funds of their affiliates, once the decision on the gross capital contribution less repatriated dividends is determined, as a foreign source of financing.

The economically interesting question for the balance of payments, especially in the short run, would appear to be which currency is used to pay for the affiliate's assets. If the

---

[54] Philip Berlin, *Foreign Affiliate Financial Survey, 1966-69*, Office of Foreign Direct Investments, US Dept. of Commerce, July 1971.

parent company is exporting its home-currency funds, the balance of payments' impact is obviously different than if foreign currency funds, whether *borrowed* or *owned* by the affiliate, are used.

Like Stevens, Ladenson, in an article written in 1972, employs a balance sheet approach within a portfolio optimization context.[55] A model of the determinants of the rate of foreign direct investments and interactions of a number of asset and liability changes are examined. A sources and uses of funds identity with five assets and two liabilities is postulated with a vector of equilibrium values towards which the model adjusts along conventional stock-adjustment lines.

The Ladenson model is empirical. The theoretical specification of the model is not discussed. After searching for proxy variables to explain the asset equations, Ladenson looks for the determinants of the liability flows, parent-company funds and foreign funds, using the same distinction as Stevens above (with the same weakness of combining reinvested earnings with parent-company funds). It is stipulated that the choice of funds should depend on their relative borrowing costs. The central bank discount rate is used, although a problem is created as the model is tested for US investment with the rest of the world.

Not surprisingly, the expected results of the model – that a discrepancy between actual and desired values of an asset should induce positive fund flows to help close the gap – are not supported. The Ladenson approach basically attempts to treat direct investment flows from the perspective of an unconstrained portfolio investor, allocating the balance sheet items as functions of tax and interest-rate differentials and sales. The approach demonstrates through its weaknesses the complexity of the question and, especially, the need to specify carefully the theoretical constructs of a model before proceeding with empirical tests.

Adler, in an article examining the cost of capital and the valuation of a firm in a two-country world, looks at constraints

[55] Mark Ladenson, 'A Dynamic Balance Sheet Approach to American Direct Foreign Investment', *International Economic Review*, October 1972.

on the single-pool concept when market imperfections are introduced.[56]

The proposition is examined that an MNE will generally follow the rule of viewing all sources of funds, wherever they may arise, as entering a single, worldwide pool to be allocated rationally among competing uses. It is assumed that firms will maximize their present value by borrowing funds in the market with the lowest interest rates when markets are not segmented. Returning to the Modigliani–Miller theorem, it is asserted that with market segmentation, the costs of capital are not independent of the financing mix, even though perfect competition is assumed to prevail within each capital market in isolation.

Adler's theoretical presentation raises the essential empirical point that if there is extensive segmentation of the international capital market, models developed for a single-country firm may not be applicable without considerable modification especially where joint ventures are operated. It should be noted that Adler only addresses this question of segmentation and exchange risks are not treated explicitly.

In a similar vein, Shapiro has recently investigated the financial structure and cost of capital in MNEs.[57] At the outset, it might be noted that the former question is not directly treated. The basic assumption is that the MNE finances its foreign affiliates in such a way as to minimize its incremental weighted cost of capital. Shapiro specifically distinguished between parent-company funds, reinvested earnings and depreciation, and local debt as sources of funds to finance foreign assets. After discussion of the appropriate norm for assessing an affiliate's financial structure, Shapiro postulates that an affiliate's capital structure is relevant only in so far as it affects the parent company's consolidated worldwide debt ratio. The various factors affecting this interaction are examined: parent company guarantees and consolidation, tax and regulatory factors, the riskiness of foreign

[56] Michael Adler, 'The Cost of Capital and Valuation of a Two-country Firm', *Journal of Finance*, March 1974.

[58] Alan Shapiro, 'Financial Structure and Cost of Capital in the Multinational Corporation', *Journal of Financial and Quantitative Analysis*, June 1978.

operations including political, inflation and exchange risks, diversification, investor's perceptions and joint ventures.

Shapiro's survey of the factors affecting the cost of capital to finance worldwide investments treats international investments as if they do not affect a firm's risk characteristics. It is acknowledged that to the extent that capital markets are segmented, the cost of borrowing abroad may not fully reflect exchange-rate expectations. But Shapiro concludes that the incremental effects of changes in currency values on the parent company's risk characteristics and, hence, on its cost of capital, can only be determined by examining the impact of variations in foreign earnings on variations in the firm's worldwide consolidated earnings. And these variations may be impossible to isolate conceptually and to separate out empirically from other causal factors affecting the earnings of the MNE.

Shapiro acknowledges that more work is required on the proposition of international capital market segmentation and on investor's perceptions of the riskiness of MNEs.

The Shapiro analysis treats exchange risk as affecting the variation in the consolidated earnings of the MNE. In this respect, the key impact of currency denomination is identified, but the formation of risk perceptions stemming from market segmentation remains to be explored.

Hartman, in developing a portfolio model to explain foreign direct investment and its financing, begins by assuming that risk matters, not to the individual firm, but rather to the individual asset owner. In assuming an extreme form of market perfection, it is contended that MNEs will operate in accord with the risk minimization objectives of firm owners.[58] Hartman contends that the portion of foreign investment that will be financed abroad will depend on a measure of the responsiveness of the rate of return available abroad in terms of home currency to changes in the exchange rate. He postulates that the more responsive the real flow of returns in home currency is to exchange-rate changes, the greater the incentive to borrow abroad to finance foreign

[58] David G. Hartman, 'Foreign Investment and Finance with Risk', *Quarterly Journal of Economics*, May 1979.

assets. There is, however, no discussion of the formation of exchange-rate expectations. A similar approach is used in a recent article by Goldsbrough in which an empirical model was treated.[59] His results indicate that arbitrage of interest differentials takes place through portfolio capital flows, whereas flows of direct investment are not significantly affected by interest differentials. He finds that desired borrowing abroad can be treated as a fairly stable proportion of fixed assets abroad, as in Stevens' model above.

The preceding discussion underscores the limitations of an unqualified portfolio-balance approach in explaining the determinants of the currency denominations of funds to finance foreign direct investment. Even when combined with corporate finance precepts of minimizing the cost of capital to finance balance-sheet changes, there has been a lack of realism in specifying the notion of exchange risk perceived by direct investors in using home currency to finance foreign assets. This weakness is probably due to the implicit assumption in most of the previous work that capital markets are to a large degree integrated, with free capital mobility as rational investors (no distinction made for direct investors), acting on perfect information (including probable changes in exchange rates) allocate their portfolios of assets and finance these changes.

Business Literature on the Financing of Direct Investment

In contrast, the business literature, often based on interviewing techniques and questionnaires, has long recognized the strong distinction made by parent companies between home-currency and foreign-currency funds to finance foreign assets.

For instance, in Polk *et al.*[60] it was found that 'companies seldom think in terms of company-owned funds, foreign or

---

[59] David G. Goldsbrough, 'The Role of Foreign Direct Investment in the External Adjustment Process', *IMF Staff Papers*, December 1979.

[60] Judd Polk, Irene Meister, and Lawrence Veit, *United States Production Abroad and the Balance of Payments*, New York: The Conference Board, 1968.

domestic, versus funds borrowed on the outside. Rather, most companies think in terms of US capital versus funds *generated* abroad by their foreign enterprises'.[61] The latter category of funds would include internal cash flow (earnings and depreciation allowances) and local borrowing without the guarantee of the parent company.

It was observed that once a foreign affiliate begins operations, its most important sources of funds are locally generated earnings, depreciation allowances, and local borrowing. In addition, it may, under certain circumstances, have access to foreign-currency funds generated abroad by other affiliates, usually provided in the form of inventory financing. In some cases, it may obtain funds from a parent-owned but foreign-based financing or holding company.

These discussions with businessmen produced a striking difference with the theoretical literature on the cost of capital. When a choice is made between parent-company loans and foreign borrowing to finance foreign assets, there is usually a strong preference for the foreign borrowing if it can be arranged at a reasonable cost. The notion of reasonable costs varies from company to company, but it was found that most companies are prepared to pay more for capital abroad and tend to consider the higher cost as a reasonable 'cost of cover' against exchange risks associated with future local receipts. In the great majority of cases, companies expressed the opinion that the advantages of obtaining local capital may well outweigh the higher cost. This may be due to the fact that non-financial investors do not only compare nominal interest-rate costs, but are subject to less than perfect information, high transactions costs and to exchange risks that make the nominal differential alone less of a criterion for profit-maximizing firms subject to constraints.

In a fairly typical newspaper account, it was reported that a US company, Armstrong Cork, generally tries to finance foreign investments in local currencies (even at higher nominal interest costs), so that debt incurred to build a facility is repaid in the same currency in which the plant

---

[61] Polk, Meister, and Veit, op. cit.

will earn income.[62] In an article by Plasschaert, it was observed that 'multinational corporations seek, to a large extent, host country financing for their subsidiaries' and that no maximum use of home-country financing sources appears to be made.[63]

In the Polk *et al.* study this behaviour is attributed to certain intangible or psychological factors. The most important of these, it was found, was whether the top management views the company as primarily a domestic concern or as a multinational entity. Most companies can be considered to have a domestic orientation and do not attach quite the same value to foreign earnings which are considered less of a drain on the total capital resources than the investment of home-currency funds. In the thinking of these companies, 'foreign holdings tend to be considered as a separate entity in the structure of their overall-corporate assets'.[64]

The domestic orientation of many companies may be related to their newness in dealing with foreign operations and a learning process may be involved. But the approach of regarding the initial investment as 'seed money' to be allowed to accumulate through the generation of earnings is prevalent. This view is generally attributed initially to Barlow and Wender who stated that

United States companies typically prefer to begin operations in a foreign country in a modest fashion with a small dollar investment. They expand the business within the country through reinvestment of local earnings to the greatest extent possible. They regard their foreign earnings much as a man does his winnings at the race track in that they are much more willing to utilize them than fresh dollar capital for additional foreign investment.[65]

From this point of view, the gains and losses involved are seen as distinct from the gambler's principal working activities. Penrose also contended that

[62] 'Dollar's Decline Spurs Many Firms to Avoid Deals in Foreign Funds', *Wall Street Journal*, 1st December, 1977.

[63] Sylvain Plasschaert, 'Multinational Companies and International Capital Markets', in Wilson and Scheffer (eds.), op. cit.

[64] Polk, Meister, and Veit, op. cit., page 93.

[65] E. R. Barlow and I. T. Wender, *Foreign Investment and Taxation*, Englewood Cliffs, N.J.: Prentice-Hall, Inc. 1955, page 161.

a preference for expansion through reinvested earnings is becoming increasingly characteristic of the modern corporation, and of particular interest from the point of view of foreign investment is the situation, especially favored by American firms, in which the parent company holds all, or nearly all, of the equity and permits the subsidiary to expand with its own earnings.[66]

Stevens[67] has interpreted Barlow and Wender's assertions as meaning that the expansion of already-established subsidiaries is financed exclusively out of these subsidiaries' retained earnings. As counter-evidence, Stevens shows that, for a large percentage of well-established subsidiaries, gross capital outflows from the US financed on average 14 per cent of plant and equipment expenditure (i.e. not total-asset changes) from 1959–62, and that there were net outflows (gross outflows less the reverse flow of dividends) for more than 20·per cent of the observations. But Stevens' counter-evidence reveals that net US capital outflow financed a bare fraction of fixed asset expenditure of US subsidiaries abroad and would seem to support Barlow and Wender that the reinvestment of local earnings is relied upon for expansion 'to the greatest extent possible'.

As Polk *et al.* concluded, the

one pervasive condition which influences the actions of all U.S. foreign investors, whatever their degree of international involvement and whatever their general policies on the handling of available foreign funds, is that the parent companies are owned predominantly by the U.S. nationals. Ultimately the gains from foreign investments must be translated into dollars and be reflected in the dividends received by the company's shareholders – and in the United States.[68]

Plasschaert, while acknowledging the role of institutional factors in the bias towards host-country financing, finds that 'the desire to hedge against foreign exchange risks provides the main rationale of this preference for foreign outside financing'.[69]

[66] E. T. Penrose, 'Foreign Investment and the Growth of the Firm', *Economic Journal*, June 1956, page 220.

[67] G. V. G. Stevens, 'The Determinants of Investment', in Dunning (ed.), op. cit., 1974.

[68] Polk, Meister, and Veit, op. cit., page 102.

[69] Plasschaert, in Wilson and Scheffer, op. cit., page 99.

These views, of fundamental importance to the theory presented below, are supported by the conclusions of an extensive 1973 study by the US Tariff Commission which found that 'multinationalism goes only so far, and for even the largest MNCs, the dollar remains their "home" currency, their currency of account, and the currency in which cost of their cash flow is generated'.[70]

Two further business studies of an empirical nature lend further support for this understanding.

In their basic text on the management of international operations,[71] Brooke and Remmers found that, at least in the larger companies, a direct or meaningful link between specific sources and uses of funds would not usually be possible. With the choice of assets determined by commercial considerations, they classify the finance available to foreign affiliates under two broad headings 'according to where it originates'. These are, (a) local sources of finance – the cash flow generated by the local operations, and the external finance obtained in the host country, and (b) foreign sources of finance – those obtained outside the host country (primarily parent-company funds).

Brooke and Remmers find that 'the bulk of funds employed by subsidiaries to finance their various needs are from local sources'.[72] More specifically, the largest single source of funds is from internal cash flow, consisting of reinvested earnings and depreciation allowances, which provided on average about 60 per cent of financing sources in their sample.[73] The second largest source of funds is local external finance which includes funds raised through the sale of securities, borrowings from financial institutions and other organizations, grants from governmental or regional authorities, and increases in trade credit, tax liabilities, and various

---

[70] US Tariff Commission for the Committee on Finance, US Senate, *Implications of Multinational Firms for World Trade and Investment and for United States Trade and Labour*, 93rd Congress, 1st Session, Washington: February 1973, page 486.

[71] M. Z. Brooke and H. L. Remmers, *The Strategy of Multinational Enterprise*, London: Longman, 1971.   [72] Ibid., page 151.

[73] Based on balance sheet data for 115 American and European subsidiaries operating in the UK from 1960 to 1967.

other items. Normally, only a small proportion of funds is supplied directly or indirectly by the parent company. Although the currency composition of funds is not discussed, it is presumed that parent-company funds are usually denominated in home-country currency.

Likewise, Robbins and Stobaugh, in their study as part of the Harvard Business School Project,[74] reached similar conclusions. Referring to the reluctance of parent companies to invest their own funds in foreign operations, they find that

> there is much evidence to support this pattern, for indeed most foreign subsidiaries were started with a modest sum. After the initial incubation period, retained earnings and depreciation allowances are the dominant source of funds, and these sources, when coupled with local borrowing, leave relatively little need for fresh funds from headquarters.[75]

The notion of Exchange Rate Illusion

This survey, thus far, reveals that the economic literature has not correctly specified the notion of risk resulting from capital-market segmentation in the theories developed to explain capital flows to finance foreign direct investment. On the other hand, the business literature appears to describe the essential characteristics of this financing behaviour – the distinction between home-country and foreign funds – but without providing a theoretical basis which would explain such behaviour. One feature, however, that both the economic and business literature appear to agree upon is the importance of exchange risk in determining the capital flows financing foreign operations. The exchange risk that is usually discussed is that associated with the value in home currency of foreign assets. Relatively little attention has been devoted to the notion of exchange risk concerning liabilities to finance these assets.

A notable exception is a 1973 article by Charles Kindleberger dealing with 'exchange rate illusion'[76] that develops

---

[74] Robbins and Stobaugh, 1973, op. cit.   [75] Ibid., page 59.

[76] C. P. Kindleberger, 'Money Illusion and Foreign Exchange', in C. F. Bergsten and W. G. Tyler, *Leading Issues in International Policy*, Lexington, Mass.: D. C. Heath, 1975.

further his ideas on this subject which were written in the 1960s.[77] Kindleberger suggests that money functions effectively, in the international context as well as domestic, only under conditions of stability such as to justify the 'illusion' that wealth and income measured in money are equivalent to real wealth and real income respectively. Money illusion is seen not as a sign of irrationality but rather, that its absence is a symptom of monetary pathology. This leads to the conclusion that, in normal times, domestic firms with foreign operations regard all currencies outside the home country as subject to risk, but not the home currency.

Kindleberger notes that increasing sophistication in the handling of international corporate finance does not yet reach to the advocacy of regarding net current assets in the home-country currency as exposed, and at risk. So long as that degree of sophistication does not exist, 'exchange-rate illusion' will be present to some extent.

The implications for the liability side of the balance sheet are significant. In a world in which exchange rates do not necessarily reflect the relative real values of currency and, more important, in which investors do not view their home currency, the numéraire, as being subject to risk, there may be a reluctance to use home-country funds which are risk free to finance foreign-currency assets which are viewed as subject to exchange risk. The consequence for national investors maximizing their wealth in terms of home-country currency is that real wealth may be at a suboptimal point.

---

[77] C. P. Kindleberger, 1966, op. cit.

V   CAPITAL FLOWS TO BE CONSIDERED

As observed in Chapter I, the capital flows examined here include both those generally labelled 'direct investment' in the balance of payment sense, using the definition of the IMF Balance of Payments Manual, 4th Edn,[1] as well as the borrowing by foreign affiliates from foreign sources and other forms of cash flow internal to affiliates (i.e. depreciation provisions and locally-generated profits).

In this broader, balance-sheet sense, the flow of direct investment is a measure of the change in the ownership position of the home country − or the change in the net worth of the home country − in the foreign affiliates of home-country enterprises; the stock corresponding to this flow (defined herein as annual stock changes) can be called the stock of direct investments or the value of direct investments abroad, labelled $\Sigma_i\Sigma_j\Sigma_k A_{ijk}$ in this study, the value of the sum of total assets, A, in the ith currency and in the jth country of the k enterprises. The focus is on the behaviour of an individual multinational enterprise so the k subscript will not be retained. Assuming realistically that the consolidated financial statements are expressed in terms of home currency, for example, the US dollar, the sum of foreign assets of an enterprise, $\Sigma_i\Sigma_j A_{ij}$, can be expressed in dollar terms by multiplying by the respective exchange rate e_i, the average annual spot rate, yielding $A_o = \Sigma_i\Sigma_j e_i A_{ij}$ where A_o is the total assets of the MNE expressed in dollars (with $e_o = 1$ for

[1] 'Direct investment refers to investment that is made to acquire a lasting interest in an enterprise operating in an economy other than that of the investor, the investor's purpose being to have an effective voice in the management of the enterprise', *Balance of Payments Manual*, 4th Edition, IMF, 1977. In practice, this is usually limited to equity participations and long-term loans provided by the parent company to its foreign affiliates.

dollar-denominated assets). It is argued that firms do not try to protect the home-currency value of their total assets, but rather they focus on the choice of currency for financing additions to assets in various countries. This concentration on asset changes stems both from accounting conventions which value stocks of assets at their historic costs and from the notion of the financing of previously acquired assets as sunk costs. In other words, the perception of currency risk exposure is high with respect to current transactions, whereas accounting exposure receives less attention.

The flow of liabilities financing the changes in assets held abroad can, from a balance sheet perspective, be divided into three separate components, each of which needs to be explained:

1. net capital flows from the home country in home-country currency, V'_{oj}, which equals the gross capital contribution, V_{oj}, less repatriated dividends, DP_{oj}. By definition, capital outflows from the home country are expressed in home-currency terms as are repatriated profits so that $e_o = 1$, the o subscript denoting home currency. This formulation of V'_{oj} corresponds to Stevens' expression, $NKO - DIV$ (p. 45);
2. net borrowing from foreign sources in foreign currency, F_{ij}, including any changes in foreign equity participations, expressed in terms of home currency by multiplying through by the appropriate exchange rate, e_i; and
3. net cash flows of the foreign affiliate, N_{ij}, which equals total profits Π_{ij}, plus depreciation allowances, DEP_{ij}. As these financing sources are generated abroad in terms of foreign currency, they are also expressed in home currency by multiplying through by e_i.

In order to keep the exposition perfectly general at this stage, the currency and country subscripts, i and j respectively, are maintained. This would imply that any ith currency could be used in any jth country to finance foreign assets. In Chapter VI, a theory is developed which shows that generally balance-sheet relationships will tend towards $i = j$.

In the following, the US dollar is expressed as the home currency where the e_i are the dollar exchange rates for the i currencies with $e_o = 1$.

The net flow of home currency capital to finance foreign direct investment, V'_{oj}, and the other sources of foreign-asset financing, constitute a subset of the numerous alternative methods for financing asset changes of foreign affiliates. It will be argued that there are causal relationships between the changes in assets and the accompanying financial flows. The accounting identity linking the changes in the value of assets (ΔA) to changes (flows) in the various liability and net worth accounts can be set out as follows:

$$e(\Delta K + \Delta I + \Delta R + \Delta LA) = V + e(F + \Delta E) \qquad (1)$$

where ΔK denotes the change in net value of plant and equipment, ΔI is the change of value of inventories, ΔR is the change in the value of gross receivables, ΔLA is the change in value of liquid assets, V denotes the fund flows in home-country currency, F is the flow of funds in foreign currency (mainly in the currency of the country in which the affiliate operates), and where ΔE is the change in the value of equity of the affiliate denominated in terms of foreign currency. The above balance-sheet changes from period $t - 1$ to t are stipulated as annual flows.

For the reasons presented on pp. 59–60, it is not necessary to add exchange-rate changes times the value of the stock of assets to equation (1) in order to derive the sources and uses identity. A non-financial firm with on-going foreign operations will generally view past investments as a sunk cost. By its nature, the company must make decisions to invest in and to finance new fixed and current assets in order to generate sales. What matters is the perceived return and risk of these asset and liability changes on the translated home-currency value of corporate profits. Changes in the value of the stock of foreign assets due to exchange rate changes are a result of accounting conventions (see pp. 15–18) so that the converted capital gains or losses do not constitute sources or uses of funds for the company. In other words, the present converted value at historic costs of foreign assets are not relevant to the current financing decisions of MNE. In addition, as balance-sheet changes are reported at the end of the year, to the extent that recent exchange-rate changes affect current financing decisions, this will be reflected in the year-end asset changes figures.

Following from equation (1) above, net fixed investment, ΔK, equals gross fixed investment, *PPE* (property, plant and equipment) minus depreciation provisions, *DEP*, or $\Delta K = PPE - DEP$; and the change in the value of equity, ΔE, equals profits, Π, minus distributed profits, *DP*. The change in equity is only relevant for the MNE as a whole expressed as $\Delta E = \Sigma_i e_i \Delta E_i$. The use of the identity to separate out distributed profits is, however, meaningful for ΔE as a source of foreign currency denominated funds to finance assets in the *i*th currency. On an aggregated basis, $\Sigma_i \Sigma_j \Delta E_{ij}$, DP_{ij} will represent payments outside the MNE as a whole to outside shareholders. Substituting these relations into equation (1), adding depreciation to both sides, yields the sources and uses identity:

$$e(PPE + \Delta I + \Delta R + \Delta LA) = V - DP + e(F + \Pi + DEP), \quad (2)$$

where $\Pi + DEP = N =$ internal cash flow of the affiliate, and where $V - DP = V' =$ net capital contribution in home currency.

It should be noted that distributed profits, *DP*, could be endogenized separately to yield a decision rule for dividend payments to head office. This would, of course, be an interesting question in itself to investigate whether certain groups of MNEs are 'remittance' or 'investment' oriented. However, the focus in the present study is on V' or $V - DP$, the net contribution of the parent company in its home currency. This formulation is due to the desire to analyse the sources of foreign-asset financing in terms of various currencies. Combining the left-hand side of the identity in (2), the various categories of assets, gives

$$\Delta A = e(PPE + \Delta I + \Delta R + \Delta LA),$$

which yields, when summing over the *i*th currencies and *j*th countries,

$$\sum_i \sum_j e_i \Delta A_{ij} = \sum_j V'_{oj} + \sum_i \sum_j e_i (F_{ij} + N_{ij}) \qquad (3)$$

The focus of the study will then be on the determinants of V'_{oj}, i.e. $(V_{oj} - DP_{oj})$, the net capital flow in home-country currency and on F_{ij}, the borrowing in foreign currency. It will be argued in Chapter VI that N_{ij}, the internal cash flow of the affiliate, is pre-determined as profits and depreciation are given by the past operations of the affiliate and cannot be varied by the financial management of the firm, at least in the short run.

VI A THEORY OF THE FINANCING OF FOREIGN DIRECT INVESTMENT

As noted in Chapter IV, virtually every observer of international business has noted that firms tend to differentiate explicitly between the financing of foreign assets in foreign currencies and in home-country currency. After an initial start, affiliates abroad must normally rely on internally generated funds and local financing through borrowing and supplier credits. Any original loan from the parent company either is turned into equity or left as an outstanding liability until the affiliate becomes sufficiently profitable to pay it off. Notwithstanding this traditional pattern, at times additional fresh parent-company funds are provided to the affiliate, sometimes to furnish needed capital when local losses have been heavy, or when there is an opportunity for faster growth and more profitable sales than internal funds alone would allow. It has been noted that this flexibility is characteristic more of medium-sized MNEs ($100–500 million annual sales) than of the larger and, especially, smaller firms with foreign operations.[1] In this context, it is usually those firms that have acquired international experience and whose foreign operations have become a significant proportion of total corporate activity which are more prepared to furnish home-currency financing to their foreign affiliates after the beginning. Even so, it was reported, for example, that a large Canadian parent company investing abroad had reiterated that it would furnish no Canadian dollars to its foreign subsidiaries.[2]

Accounting practice takes account of exposure only in

[1] Robbins and Stobaugh, 1973, op. cit., page 60.
[2] E. P. Neufeld, *A Global Corporation: A History of the International Developments of Massey-Ferguson Limited*, Toronto: University of Toronto Press, 1969, pages 16, 90, 349.

foreign exchange, and does not question the net exposed position in the currency of the home country of the parent company. Furthermore, foreign-exchange losses are reported as an exceptional item in the balance sheet, whereas capital gains on foreign exchange or the higher cost of foreign-currency debt are simply added as revenues or deducted as expenses and so are much less visible to shareholder scrutiny.

The narrow, national focus of most direct investors, at least in the earlier phases of international expansion, combined with standard accounting practices which emphasize exchange losses, are deemed to explain the formulation of exchange-risk perceptions which promote a financial stance to minimize the risk to the parent company in each currency (except that of the home country).

In international investment, a number of classifications of direct investors has been made based on their size, experience, and sophistication. One of these taxonomies distinguishes between (1) domestic firms with foreign operations; (2) multinational corporations; and (3) international corporations. In theory, the first regards its foreign investments as merely incidental to its main preoccupations in the home country; the second tries to act everywhere as a 'good citizen' of the country where it is; the third tries to maximize income and wealth worldwide without regard to nationality, whether that of the home country or those of host countries.[3] It follows that the three classes of firms would be likely to behave differently along a series of dimensions — with respect to acceptable rates of return, personnel selection for foreign affiliates, the location of research and development, reinvestment of foreign-earned profits, and a number of operating policies, including attitudes towards exchange risk. On exchange risk, it was hypothesized that domestic firms with foreign operations regard all currencies outside the home country as subject to risk, but not the home currency.

The national corporation is usually hedged in foreign exchange, is seldom long of foreign currencies, and is ready to go short when a

---

[3] C. P. Kindleberger, *American Business Abroad*, New Haven, Conn.: Yale University Press, 1969.

foreign currency is under attack. It will not take a short position in the currency of the parent company and does not, in fact, recognise that it has an exchange position when it holds net assets denominated in money in that currency.[4]

The multinational corporation would be reluctant to go short of the currency of a country where it has an investment, as this may be regarded as a breach of good citizenship. It is long of most currencies, hedged in weak ones, but like the national firm, likely to ignore the fact that it can have an exchange risk in the home currency. The international corporation, on the other hand, is aware that effective maximization of its real wealth may require it to go long or short of any currency, including that of the head office. It calculates its net worth in a single currency as numéraire, but that practice does not mean that it ignores changes in the value of that numéraire.

The degree of exchange illusion between the two former categories of firms would differ however. In the first case, not only is the home currency viewed as devoid of exchange risk but foreign currencies could be considered at risk in all cases without regard to exchange-rate expectations in individual currencies. For the multinational corporation, on the other hand, there would still be no perceived exchange risk in the home currency, but the expected home-currency values of various foreign currencies are differentiated.

Hymer had contended, as is argued in the present study, that most corporations investing abroad are national ones with foreign operations, rather than multinational companies or international firms in the sense of Kindleberger's somewhat abstract taxonomy.[5] The two latter categories are hypothetical constructs which do not seem to correspond to the actual practices of most firms at the present time. Balance sheets and profit and loss statements are denominated in national currency, equity shares are priced in it, and the corporate management is committed to maximize income

[4] Kindleberger, 1969, op. cit.
[5] Hymer, op. cit. In practice, these distinctions tend to be blurred and it may be particularly difficult to distinguish between multinational and international corporations.

and wealth in that currency only, without regard to the question of whether some other currency is stronger and that by holding it, the management would one day achieve a higher value for the firm's assets expressed in its normal numéraire. American management cannot be criticized for holding dollars, nor British management for holding sterling.

A report for the US Senate noted that the US multinational corporation operates largely in dollars, even abroad, meaning that whatever the currency used to make transactions, the reporting is made in dollars. 'The subsidiaries of U.S. ownership act as collectors of foreign exchange which they largely channel to the U.S. in dollars'.[6] Another study expressed the same national focus in the following terms: 'The attribute of foreign money of most interest from the perspective of the U.S. dollar financial statements is its command over U.S. dollars'.[7] Foreign currencies entail a risk, but not the home currency, from this point of view. Assets denominated in foreign currencies are seen as riskier in terms of home-currency profits than similar assets in the home country.

Kindleberger has noted that such behaviour 'is not patriotism but exchange illusion, which seems to be implicit in the current practice of international investment'.[8] In the above typology, both the national firm with foreign operations and the multinational company have exchange-rate illusion (i.e. the perception that wealth and income measured in a numéraire are equivalent to real wealth and real income respectively). The theory and empirical evidence presented here suggest that at the level of corporate sophistication in recent years, most companies investing abroad exhibit attitudes and adopt financing procedures which, as Heckerman contends,[9] would seem to have elements of irrationality about them and which imply the existence of exchange illusion.

[6] *Multinational Corporations in the Dollar Devaluation Crisis*, Staff Report for the Sub-Committee on Multinational Corporations, U.S. Senate, 94th Session, June 1975, page 25.

[7] Leonard Lorenson, *Reporting Foreign Operations in Dollars*, New York: American Institute of Certified Public Accountants, 1972, page 18.

[8] Kindleberger, 1975, op. cit., page 59.

[9] Heckerman, op. cit.

It may well be that, in a world of perfect information where portfolios are effectively maximized in perfectly integrated capital markets, such behaviour would seem irrational. In the real world, due to imperfect information, inelastic expectations, capital market segmentation with significant information and transactions costs, the relatively short-time horizon for most non-financial investors in relation to their need for liquid assets denominated in any currency, and the pursuit of other objectives than just portfolio maximization (long-run growth, enhancing the independence or security of management, etc.), given the risk aversion of the parent-company management, such *behaviour may be rational under present circumstances and consistent with portfolio maximization criteria subject to constraints.*

As stated in the introduction, the economically significant question for the balance of payments is why, contrary to the conclusions of numerous studies of international capital flows and of corporate finance, multinational companies appear to finance foreign assets with foreign liabilities rather than with home-currency liabilities, even taking into account exchange-rate expectations and the relative cost of debt. The monographic business literature on the optimal pattern of financing would not yet seem to have altered actual corporate behaviour beyond a certain degree. Where cost of capital and exchange-rate considerations would dictate the use of home-currency liabilities (from the point of view of the affiliate) to finance foreign assets, most companies seem to prefer to pay the higher cost of using foreign-currency financing.[10]

On the one hand, it could be hypothesized that these phenomena have little to do with operations in various currencies, but, rather, are related to the management structure and behavioural characteristics of MNEs. That is, it could be assumed that a MNE treats each of its foreign operations as

[10] Of course, the covered interest-rate differential, i.e. the difference between interest rates on comparable borrowing instruments in two different currencies, adjusted for the relevant swap rate, should be zero in theory due to interest arbitrage. In practice, as shown in the empirical tests in Chapter VII below, the divergence from zero may not be significant enough to overcome the information and transactions costs encountered by non-financial borrowers.

'autonomous' with the parent company acting merely as an international holding company. In this case, the central headquarters would instruct each overseas affiliate that, in most circumstances, it must operate independently and must raise its own funds to support any increase in assets. This polycentric structure — with the MNE as a sort of confederation of related companies — would appear to fit the observed financial behaviour described above. However, a theory which prescribes the simple minimization of all home-currency financing would not allow for the establishment or expansion of firms abroad (where the use of parent funds may be critical). Moreover, while such a hypothesis may apply in some cases, e.g. some conglomerates, it would negate the major strength of MNEs, that is inherent advantages over domestic firms which can be exploited through centrally co-ordinated operations.[11] Thus, a polycentric explanation with each affiliate following the rule of 'each tub on its own bottom' in raising funds is not interesting in terms of explanatory power of actual MNE financial operations.

Instead, a more robust hypothesis is suggested. The reasoning underlying this financial behaviour which constitutes the basis of the present study can be summarized as follows: most MNEs are essentially national companies with foreign operations and therefore regard assets denominated in foreign currencies as being inherently inferior, i.e. subject to greater uncertainty in terms of the value in home currency and subject to actual or potential costs not associated with domestic assets. The approximate maximization of nominal worldwide profits in terms of home currency (assumed to correspond to the nominal increase in the wealth of shareholders) is perceived by management as being subject to greater risk if shareholders' funds (reserves) or debt (leveraged on shareholders funds) are used to finance risky foreign-currency asset accumulation. A MNE maximizing its profits would perceive the income stream for foreign currency denominated assets as being subject to a random variable, e, the exchange rate, so that an extra risk factor is attached to

[11] See, for instance, N. Hood and S. Young, *The Economics of the Multinational Enterprise*, London: Longman, 1979, Chapter 14.

foreign assets (given) and to foreign liabilities. This limited perception could also be expressed as the notion that a MNE attaches a liquidity premium to its home country which it considers as money, but considers foreign currencies as if they were commodities.[12]

This 'risk reduction' hypothesis is based upon the view that firms wish to minimize the variance of profits in home-currency terms (especially negative variations because of the explicit accounting treatment of exchange losses) due to random changes in bilateral, nominal exchange rates, i.e. of each foreign currency *vis-à-vis* the home-country currency. Some further elaboration of these concepts may be useful as it may not be readily apparent that wealth maximization or the consideration of exchange rates as random variables are realistic assumptions.

With respect to the wealth maximization assumption, two questions are raised: is such an assumption realistic and to what extent is it necessary for the theory developed herein? As noted on p. 14, this assumption is in general use in the literature, but is it really true that MNEs attempt to maximize wealth, or, rather, is this just a theoretical tool for simpler exposition? It would be difficult to contend that corporate behaviour is perfectly 'rational' in this special sense, even though large, quoted companies are under closer scrutiny by the market, regulatory authorities and potential predators for deviations from wealth maximization than some smaller firms with less public exposure. In fact, as stated on p. 63, there will be several constraints on the corporate management which will impede the sole pursuit of growth of net assets. These constraints stem from the fact that the perfect market assumed, explicitly or implicitly, in portfolio and even in corporate finance models may not exist in reality. The 'exchange illusion' postulated in the theoretical model below is another example of the 'real world' constraints

[12] Given the market segmentation perceived by non-financial investors due to significant information and transactions costs, assets denominated in foreign currencies can be viewed as commodities in the sense that their converted value in home-currency terms at a future date is subject to uncertainty. This uncertainty may be reduced with the growing sophistication of non-financial investors as argued on pp. 72–3.

which make corporate behaviour appear to be irrational. Therefore, in response to the first point, wealth maximization is a simplifying assumption, but it can be used to explain real behaviour in most cases so long as the constraints are clearly retained in the exposition and interpretation of the model.

As to the second aspect, i.e. whether the assumption is necessary to the development of the theory below, wealth maximization does not apply to the 'risk reduction' hypothesis except in a limited sense which would seem to correspond to actual corporate financial behaviour. It should be remembered that the theoretical model presented here is *not* a general hypothesis of MNE behaviour, but, rather, it only attempts to explain one particular aspect of this behaviour, which is the currency sources of liability changes financing *given* foreign-asset changes. Whether firms maximize wealth or pursue alternative goals in acquiring foreign assets is not strictly relevant to the present model. Therefore, the wealth maximization assumption is only necessary to an analysis of the foreign-financing function. In this limited sense, such an assumption seems to be realistic. In most non-financial companies, the financial function is subjugated to the operational aspects of the firm and the financial managers are generally assigned the task of making low-risk funds available at minimum costs to finance a given quantity of assets. The scope for pursuing alternative objectives is necessarily limited.

Concerning the treatment of bilateral, nominal exchange rates as random variables, similar questions as to realism and the necessity of such an assumption are raised. The focus here is on the bilateral, nominal exchange rate of each foreign currency *vis-à-vis* the home currency. If, instead, the focus was on the 'real' exchange rate (i.e. the nominal rate adjusted for inflation differentials), it would become much more difficult to argue that the rate is a random variable. And even the seeming randomness of the nominal rate could be undermined once it is explicitly recognized that there is a systematic relationship between interest-rate differentials and forward and spot rates (i.e. interest parity). In response, however, it should be noted that purchasing-power parity and interest parity are concepts which are deemed to hold in the longer run, but which may have very limited relevance to short-run financial decisions. In addition, although it could be asserted that many managers understand these concepts, the use of such notions implies a degree of sophistication which would be uncommon for non-financial companies, at least prior to the widespread floating of rates. In fact, corporate accounting rules have generally discouraged an appraisal of 'real' exposure (primarily due to a lack of inflation accounting so that financial statements still focus on nominal accounts). Furthermore, it should be noted that no distinction is made with respect to exchange-rate expectations as such, but rather to foreign-currency assets in general whether the specific bilateral rate is expected to rise or fall. With time, however, national firms with foreign operations may develop to another level of sophistication, taking expectations of exchange-rate changes, even eventually of the home currency, into consideration. This learning process over time is postulated as being highly significant.

If 'exchange-rate illusion' is a result of market imperfections as perceived by non-financial investors, then it is apparent that, in a dynamic context, developments in market structures, government regulations and, perhaps most important, changing cost considerations will lead to a reduction in 'exchange-rate illusion', and will occur when the expenditures to overcome market imperfections are viewed as marginally less than the costs of continued exchange illusion to rational, profit-maximizing firms. This learning process in which MNEs require greater financial sophistication may follow, in part, from the increasing efficiency of financial markets (e.g., lower transaction costs, better financial-management techniques, etc.) and also from the possibly higher costs of accepting 'exchange-rate illusion' when exchange rates are volatile in both directions against the home currency, as would be the case since the introduction of generalized floating exchange rates since 1973.

Moreover, just as the occurrence of 'exchange-rate illusion' between MNEs of the same parent country may vary, so it is also likely that 'exchange-rate illusion' will differ between MNEs of various countries and industries. For instance, it is likely that European-based MNEs, particularly in the smaller countries such as the Netherlands and Switzerland, are less subject to 'exchange-rate illusion' among various currencies, and even in their home currencies, than US-based MNEs. This difference in perception would be due to both lower market segmentation (very open economies, a high degree of trade and financial inter-penetration, cultural familiarity and, in some cases, similar institutional arrangements and management styles) and, especially, to the greater costs of accepting 'exchange-rate illusion' in a very open economy whose money is not an international medium of exchange and store of value (i.e. a 'key money'). Recent European initiatives to stabilize exchange rates in the European Monetary System, however, may work in the other direction by lowering the potential costs of 'exchange-rate illusion' (provided, of course, that rates are actually stabilized).

Finally, the specification of the exchange rate as a random variable has been chosen in the belief that most non-financial companies, at least in the earlier stages of international expansion, have viewed the home-currency value of foreign assets as being beyond their control and whose timing and even direction and magnitude of changes are exceedingly difficult to predict. Hence, the choice of a random variable is an approximation of this view. With all due respect to the problem of choosing assumptions to conform to *a priori* predictions, the model developed herein is simple enough to indicate that the existence of 'exchange illusion' is symptomatic of a lack of interest parity and purchasing-power parity considerations on the part of most of these firms. To the extent that non-financial companies have been or are becoming more aware of these considerations, a decline in 'exchange illusion' would indicate that firms can anticipate home-currency values of foreign assets and so treat the exchange rate as endogenous.

Continuing now with the 'risk-reduction' hypothesis outlined on p. 70, the objective function of the financial management of a MNE is to invest home-currency funds only to the point that *minimizes total risk to the parent company in foreign currencies.* Another way of stating this is that home-currency funds will be leveraged against foreign funds to the point that the marginal cost of such action equals the marginal revenue. It is assumed that in the short run the direct investment decision itself, i.e. what amount of assets to invest where, is already made. The MNE then decides how to finance a given level of assets in each currency. This approach separating the investment and financing decisions, which is described on p. 92, is pervasive in the corporate-finance literature.[13] In reality, asset and liability decisions are interwoven to some extent, particularly with respect to those investment choices where the availability and cost of finance may be an important constraint. This assumption, however, one of partial equilibrium, is useful for expositional purposes to assess the prime determinants governing the financing of direct investment. It is assumed that the financing decisions are independent of one another which entails a separability assumption which states that inter-affiliate flows of funds are insignificant. This assumption will not hold in all sectors and at all times, but would seem to be generally applicable to many manufacturing MNEs.

Such a relationship can be expressed in a general form, using the accounting identity in equation (3) of Chapter V and including the exchange rate to place the identity in home-currency terms where $e_o = 1$, as

$$\sum_i \sum_j e_i \Delta A_{ij} = \sum_i \sum_j e_i \Delta L_{ij} \qquad (4)$$

where ΔA_{ij} is changes in assets (uses of funds) and ΔL_{ij} is changes in liabilities (sources of funds). e_i is the exchange rate with the subscripts denoting the ith currency and the jth country.

On the assets side of equation (4), it is possible to be more specific as the assets acquired by a non-financial company in any country will be assumed to be denominated in the curency of that country so that $i = j$ for all assets, such that

[13] See Goldsbrough, op. cit. and G. V. G. Stevens, 'Capital Mobility and the International Firm', in Machlup, Salant, and Tarshis (eds.), 1972, op. cit.

$$\sum_i \sum_j e_i \Delta A_{ij} = \sum_j e_j \Delta A_{jj}$$

On the liability side, however, liabilities in the jth country may be financed with the ith currencies. Using the separability theorem, the choice will generally be to finance foreign assets with jth-currency liabilities in the jth country or with home-currency liabilities. Financing of an affiliate in the jth country can be viewed as follows,

$$\sum_j e_j \Delta A_{jj} = \sum_j \Delta L_{oj} + \sum_j e_j \Delta L_{jj} + \sum_i \sum_j e_i \Delta L_{ij} \qquad (5)$$

where i does not equal j or the home currency. In other words, foreign-asset changes can be financed in the jth country with home currency, jth currency, or some other ith currency. The last term is deemed to be insignificant. So, without any loss of specificity, liability changes can be expressed as in equation (4) as,

$$\sum_{i=0}^{J} \sum_{j=0}^{J} e_i \Delta L_{ij} = \sum_{j=0}^{J} \Delta L_{oj} + \sum_{j=1}^{J} e_j \Delta L_{jj} + \sum_{i=1}^{J} \sum_{j=1}^{J} e_i \Delta L_{ij}.$$

Therefore, equation (4) can be expressed as:

$$1 = \frac{\sum_i \sum_j e_i \Delta L_{ij}}{\sum_j e_j \Delta A_{jj}}$$

sources and uses must sum to unity. This can then be re-written using equation (5) as,

$$\frac{\sum_i \sum_j e_i \Delta L_{ij}}{\sum_j e_j \Delta A_{jj}} = \sum_j \left[\frac{\Delta L_{oj} e_j \Delta A_{jj}}{e_j \Delta A_{jj} \sum_j e_j \Delta A_{jj}} \right] + \sum_j \left[\frac{e_j \Delta L_{jj} e_j \Delta A_{jj}}{e_j \Delta A_{jj} \sum_j e_j \Delta A_{jj}} \right]$$

$$+ \frac{\sum_i \sum_j e_i \Delta L_{ij}}{\sum_j e_j \Delta A_{jj}}. \qquad (7)$$

That is, asset changes in the jth country denominated in the *j*th currency can be financed with home-currency liabilities, *j*th-currency liabilities or *i*th-currency liabilities. For the MNE as a whole, this expression can be more specifically written as,

$$\frac{\sum_i \sum_j e_i \Delta L_{ij}}{\sum_j e_j \Delta A_{jj}} = \left\{ \frac{\Delta L_{oo}}{\Delta A_{oo}} \frac{\Delta A_{oo}}{\sum_j e_j \Delta A_{jj}} + \sum_{j=0} \left[\frac{\Delta L_{oj}}{e_j \Delta A_{jj}} \frac{e_j \Delta A_{jj}}{\sum_j e_j \Delta A_{jj}} \right] \right\}$$

$$+ \left\{ \sum_{j \neq 0} \left[\frac{\Delta L_{jj}}{\Delta A_{jj}} \frac{e_j \Delta A_{jj}}{\sum_j e_j \Delta A_{jj}} \right] \right\} + \frac{\sum_i \sum_j e_i \Delta L_{ij}}{\sum_j e_j \Delta A_{jj}} . (8)$$

The first term within brackets on the right-hand side denotes that home-currency liabilities can be used to finance changes in home-currency denominated assets, ΔA_{oo}, weighted by the proportion of home currency assets to total asset changes (calling $\Delta A_{oo}/(\Sigma_j e_j \Delta A_{jj}) = \omega_{oo}$) or changes in *j*th-country assets where $j \neq 0$. The second term in brackets denotes the use of *j*th-currency liabilities to finance changes in *j*th-currency denominated assets times the weighting, ω_{jj}, of *j*th assets in total-asset changes. The last term on the right-hand side denotes the possibility of using some third-country currency liabilities to finance asset changes in *j*. Except for normal, short-term trade credits, the separability assumption would dictate that this latter term, the ω_{ij} weighting, will be insignificant. Re-writing equation (8) using the weighting of assets terms,

$$\frac{\sum_i \sum_j e_i \Delta L_{ij}}{\sum_j e_j \Delta A_{ij}} = \frac{\Delta L_{oo}}{\Delta A_{oo}} \omega_{oo} + \sum_{j \neq 0} \left[\frac{\Delta L_{oj}}{e_j \Delta A_{jj}} + \frac{e_j \Delta L_{jj}}{e_j \Delta A_{jj}} \right] \omega_{jj}$$

$$+ \sum_i \sum_{j \neq 0} \frac{e_j \Delta L_{ij}}{e_j \Delta A_{jj}} \omega_{ij}.$$

With the last term of ω_{ij} being insignificant, however, it can

be written as a residual, u, assuming that the financing decisions of the j affiliates are independent. Then, using the more
specific notations of Chapter V,

$$\frac{\sum_i \sum_j e_i \Delta L_{ij}}{\sum_j e_j \Delta A_{jj}} = \frac{\Delta L_{oo}}{\Delta A_{oo}} \omega_{oo} + \sum_{j=1}^{J} \left[\frac{V_i' + e_j F_j}{e_j \Delta A_{jj}} \omega_{jj} \right] + u. \quad (9)$$

From a general point of view, equation (9) expresses the
risk-reduction theory of international operations as a
function of the degree of 'exchange-rate illusion' on the part
of direct investors. The various weighting terms express the
parent-company's perception of risk of financing jth-currency
assets with ith-currency liabilities. The risk-reduction hypothesis would stipulate that ω_{ij} shall be insignificant when
$i \neq j$, and that the ω_{ij} term will tend towards unity when
$i = j$. The weighting, which essentially reflects the degree of
exchange-rate illusion of parent companies, provides indirect
evidence of the extent of capital-market segmentation perceived by direct investors. This view of the financial operations of MNEs would contend that the use of global
corporate 'cash' pooling and of extensive multilateral
financial relations (i.e. using any ith currency in the matrix
of the system to finance any jth currency-denominated asset)
is not characteristic of the actual operations of most non-
financial MNEs.

In fact, the above formulation with ω_{ij}, $i \neq j$, being insignificant, would imply that the financial relations of most
MNEs are *bilateral* between the parent company and each
affiliate. The net parent-company financing V', and the
foreign borrowing, F, decisions will be taken separately in
relation to each foreign affiliate. Using Kindleberger's
taxonomy (see p. 66) it could be said that the various ω_{ij}s
correspond to different stages of the international development and sophistication of companies. National companies
with foreign operations, the prime focus in the present study,
have exchange illusion in both home and foreign currencies,
so pursuing an ω_{oj} strategy – home-currency liabilities, L_o,
will not generally be used to finance jth asset changes.

Multinational companies will perceive different risks in various currencies but not in home currency, whereas the international corporation would theoretically employ liabilities in any ith currency to finance any jth currency-denominated assets. These patterns can also be portrayed diagramatically. In Fig. 1, a national company with foreign operations pursues bilateral relationships with its affiliates abroad. The parent company centralizes all financial flows with relatively little autonomy delegated to the local management in this field. Such a pattern implies the perception by non-financial investors of a high degree of segmentation between national capital markets.

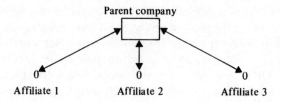

Fig. 1   Diagram A

At the other extreme is the international corporation portrayed in Fig. 2 in which market segmentation is low so that non-financial investors would operate as other portfolio managers, using liabilities in any ith currency to finance assets denominated in any jth currency. Rational expectations based on interest-rate and exchange-rate considerations would determine the amounts and direction of capital flows.

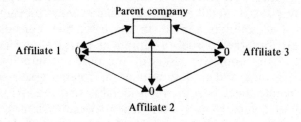

Fig. 2   Diagram B

The Notion of Risk and the Financing of Foreign Operations

In order to derive the determinants of the financing to foreign operations (i.e. the three sources of funds in equation (4) V'_{oj}, F_{ij} and N_{ij}), it is essential to understand the concept of risk expectations expressed by ω_{ij}.

The perception of risk is that as the return and capital gains on foreign-currency assets are denominated in that currency, the increasing amount of home currency used to finance a given level of foreign-asset accumulation will increase proportionately the expected variance of the return and capital gains in the home currency.

Initially, it is assumed that there are no assets abroad and normally some home currency must be invested in foreign assets in order to generate foreign-currency net worth and the capacity for local financing for further asset accumulation abroad. There are frequent occasions when local sources of finance are either insufficient, inappropriate or simply un-available to finance the acquisition of assets. When a foreign affiliate is first established or purchased, for instance, there will be, by definition, no internal cash flow nor will local lenders be prepared to supply credit where the 'track record' of the borrower is not established. In terms of the parent-company balance sheet, the small amount of home-currency assets committed to begin with will be insignificant and consistent with portfolio maximization (and diversifica-tion) to minimize overall parent-company risk. It was such considerations that led Barlow and Wender to contend that direct investors regard their foreign investments as a gamble, i.e. they put up a small amount of stake money to begin with and let it accumulate abroad. In any case, they consider the assets attributable to such a gamble as marginal and as sub-sidiary to the domestic assets of the parent company. It is only over time and as the amount of foreign assets in the total balance sheet becomes considerable that the attitude of the parent company may alter. When foreign-currency assets are no longer regarded as marginal to the parent, but still subsidiary to domestic assets (i.e. riskier), then a firm may be said to be in transition from a national company with foreign operations to becoming a multinational enterprise. At the same time, with growing international experience and awareness, and developments in the sophistication and integration of capital markets, the firm may take a less parochial view of exchange risk — reaching an understanding that the higher cost of foreign-currency funds (in some cases) may not be commensurate with the risk to parent-company home-currency profits. This would still not imply that a possible exchange position in the home currency would be appreciated.

Risk from the point of view of the parent company is equated with the *variance of profits in terms of home currency of operations in the* i*th currency and the* j*th country*, where profits include both operating profits and capital gains. The hypothesis is that the parent company tries to minimize this variance subject to its balance sheet constraint,

$$1 = \frac{\sum_i \sum_j e_i \Delta L_{ij}}{\sum_j e_j A_{jj}} \tag{6}$$

It is assumed that the parent company has already chosen its optimal level of current and fixed assets, labour and output so as to maximize its market value. The activities of an industrial company essentially set up flows of resources which move from production to sales, and thence back through research, marketing and investment, to further production. To carry out these activities, a profit-maximizing firm will invest in assets so as to optimize expected profits. The amounts and distribution of assets between fixed assets, inventories, trade credits, liquid assets, etc., will be determined by the sales prospects of the company, its existing earnings performance and the technical relationship between desired sales and required proportions of various assets.

Subject to these predetermined variables, the firm then determines its financing of foreign assets so as to minimize the risk of exchange fluctuations of profits in terms of home currency.

FFDI - G

To simplify matters, the following further assumptions are made:

1. The only random variable the firm faces is the exchange rate in each market, e_j (as described on pp. 72–3). The home market is numbered 0, and $e_0 = 1$.
2. The firm minimizes its risk in each period by redeploying its financing arrangements rather than through hedging activities.[14]

From equation (2) above, worldwide profits in terms of home currency can be expressed as,

$$\sum_i e_i \Pi_i = \sum_i \sum_j \left[e_i (\Delta A_{ij} - F_{ij} - DEP_{ij}) - V_{oj} + DP_{oj} \right]$$

in which profits are expressed in terms of changes in balance-sheet relationships, from the identity,

$$\sum_i e_i \Delta A_j = \sum_i \sum_j (e_i F_{ij} + e_i N_{ij} + V_{oj} - DP_{oj})$$

with

$$\sum_i \sum_j e_i N_{ij} = \sum_i \sum_j (e_i \Pi_{ij} + e_i DEP_{ij}).$$

V_{oj} and DP_{oj} are already expressed in home currency as parent company capital contributions and dividends are paid in home currency.

The objective is to derive decision rules for foreign-asset financing in the current period. At the beginning of the period, the asset acquisition decisions have been taken and so the objective is to determine $e_i F_{ij}$, and $V_{oj} - DP_{oj}$ (or V'_{oj}). So, it is postulated that the profit at risk is derived from

---

[14] This assumption seems to be realistic as the use of the forward exchange market by direct investors is normally limited to cover trade receivables or payables. The cost of forward cover, especially when it is most needed, is a deterrent, as well as there being government interventions and regulations limiting its availability in some cases (see pp. 18–19).

$$\sum_i e_i \Pi_i = \sum_i \sum_j [e_i(\Delta A_{ij} - F_{ij} - DEP_{ij}) - V_{oj} + DP_{oj}]$$

The parent company wishes to minimize the risk of the home-currency value of total profits. Variance is the measure the firm chooses as the indicator of risk. Assuming, for simplicity, that the firm expects no correlations among exchange-rate changes in different currencies (see p. 72), the overall variance, or risk of total profits is

$$VAR = \sum_i var \, e_i(\Delta A_i - F_i - DEP_i)^2.$$

The exchange risk of total profits is perceived as a function of the currency denominations of the balance-sheet changes, irrespective of their location which is given by the balance-sheet constraints. Hence the j subscript is not retained in the definition of variance which is then minimized subject to the firm's balance sheet,

$$\sum_j e_j(A_j - D_j - \text{net worth}_j)_t - \sum_t \sum_j (V_j - DP_j)_t = B_t = 0$$

where D is total debt outstanding and where net worth is constant. This identity holds, so that $B_t = B_{t-1} + \Delta B_t$, the balance sheet must balance at the end of each period, hence

$$\Delta B_t = 0.$$

In currency terms, and with $(A_j - D_j - \text{net worth}_j) = Z_j$,

$$\Delta B_t = \Delta B_{ot} + \sum_{j=1}^{J} \Delta B_{jt}$$

where

$$\sum_{j=1}^{J} \Delta B_{jt} = \Delta \sum_t \sum_j e_j Z_{jt} + \sum_j \sum_t V'_{jt},$$

such that

$$\Delta B_t = \Delta B_{ot} + \sum_j e_j Z_j + \sum_j Z_j \Delta e_j + \sum_j \Delta e_j \Delta Z_j + \sum_j V'_{jt}$$

$$= \Delta B_{ot} + \sum_j e_{jt-1}(\Delta A_j - N_j - F_j)$$

$$+ \sum_j \Delta e_{jt}(A_j - D_j - NW_j)_{t-1} + \sum_j V'_{jt}$$

$$+ \sum_j \Delta e_{jt}(\Delta A_j - N_j - F_j),$$

or
$$= \Delta B_{ot} + \sum_j e_{jt}(\Delta A_j - N_j - F_j) +$$

$$+ \sum_j \Delta e_{jt}(A_j - D_j - NW_j)_{t-1} + \sum_j V'_{jt}$$

with the second term on the right-hand side expressing exchange rate changes on previous acquisitions which, as argued on pp. 59–60, will be insignificant.

Thus, the balance sheet for each affiliate must balance in each time period t. If the balance-sheet constraint holds in each period, then so does ΔB which equals zero. So liabilities are issued during the course of each period, t, subject to $B_t = 0$.[15]

[15] It becomes apparent that balance sheet relationships are the same as those in equation (9) above, i.e.

$$\frac{\sum_i \sum_j e_j L_{ij}}{\sum_j e_j \Delta A_{jj}} = \frac{\Delta L_{oo}}{\Delta A_{oo}} \omega_{oo} + \sum_{j \neq 0}^{J} \left\{ \frac{V_j + e_j F_j}{e_j \Delta A_{jj}} \omega_{jj} \right\} + u$$

which can be rewritten as

$$\frac{\sum_i \sum_j e_i L_{ij}}{\sum_j e_j \Delta A_{jj}} = \omega_{oo} \left\{ \frac{\Delta B_{oo}}{\Delta A_{oo}} - 1 \right\} + \sum_j \omega_{jj} \left\{ \frac{\Delta B_{jj}}{\Delta A_{jj}} - 1 \right\} + u$$

Using the objective function on p. 83),

$$\Pi = \sum_{j=0}^{J} e_j \Pi_j$$

and where the variance is

$$\text{var } \Pi = \text{var} \sum_{j=0}^{J} e_j \Pi_j$$

$$= \text{var}(e_0 \Pi_0 + e_1 \Pi_1 + e_2 \Pi_2 \ldots + e_J \Pi_J)$$

$$= (e_0 \Pi_0 + e_1 \Pi_1 + e_2 \Pi_2 \ldots + e_J \Pi_J)^2$$

$$= \Pi_0^2 \text{var } e_0 + \Pi_1^2 \text{var } e_1 + \Pi_2^2 \text{var } e_2 + \ldots$$

$$+ \Pi_j^2 \text{var } e_j + 2 \sum_J \sum_{J'} \text{cov } e_{J'} e_J \Pi_{J'J}.$$

If $e_0 = 1$, then the firm has exchange illusion. Using the separability assumption, it is assumed that cov $e_{j'} e_j = 0$. Accepting that cov $e_{j'} e_j = 0$, which is similar to rejecting

$$\frac{\sum_i \sum_j e_i \Delta L_{ij}}{\sum_j e_j \Delta A_{jj}}$$

on p. 81 and minimizing, using the Lagrangian multiplier,

---

which is derived from the fact that

$$\frac{V_j^i + e_j F_j}{\Delta A_{jj}} = \Delta A_j - \Delta B_j$$

$$= \frac{\Delta B_j - \Delta A_j}{\Delta A_j}$$

$$\pounds = \sum_j \text{var } e_j(\Delta A_j - F_j - DEP_j)^2$$

$$+ \lambda[B_{ot} + \sum_j e_{jt}(\Delta A_j - N_j - F_j)$$

$$+ \sum_j \Delta e_{jt}(A_j - D_j - NW_j)_{t-1} - \sum_j V'_{jt}]$$

yields the following first-order conditions:

$$\frac{\partial \pounds}{\partial \lambda} = \Delta B_{ot} + \sum_j e_{jt}(\Delta A_j - N_j - F_j) = 0$$

and

$$\frac{\partial \pounds}{\partial V'_j} = -\lambda = 0$$

which implies that the parent company is the slack variable. This is due to the perception (i.e. 'exchange illusion') that home-currency borrowing entails no exchange risk, so that with $\lambda = 0$, the balance-sheet constraint is not binding.

$$\frac{\partial \pounds}{\partial F_j} = -2 \text{ var } e_i(\Delta A_i - F_i - DEP_i) - \lambda e_j = 0$$

as

$$\sum_i \text{var } e_i(\Delta A_i - F_i - DEP_i) = 0 \quad \text{since var } e_o = 0.$$

Since the firm has exchange illusion, $\lambda = 0$, it will perceive its desired foreign-financing arrangements as,

$$F_j^* = \Delta A_j - DEP_j \quad \text{for } j = 1, \dots, J$$

or

$$\left(\sum_i V'_{jt}\right)^* = \Delta A_j - N_j - F_j$$

$J + 1$ equations

On the other hand, in the case of an international corporation making its financing decisions (for given assets) without 'exchange illusion', i.e. $\lambda \neq 0$, then it would compare liabilities denominated in various ith currencies on a portfolio basis with the balance-sheet constraint applying.

A multinational company (but not a 'super-rational', i.e. an international corporation) will solve the $j + 1$ equations, for foreign borrowing,

$$F_j = F_j^*$$

and for net home-currency financing,

$$\sum_j V_{jt}' = \sum_j e_j(F_j^* - F_j - \Pi_j)_t + \sum_j \Delta e_{jt} Z_{jt} + \Delta B_{ot}$$

A national firm with foreign operations using bilateral relations between the parent company and each affiliate will solve the $2J + 1$ equations:[16]

$$F_j = F_j^* \qquad \text{for } j = 1, \ldots, J$$
$$V_{jt}' = e_j(F_j^* - F_j - \Pi_j)$$

$$\sum_{j=1}^{J} V_{jt}' = \sum_{j=1}^{J} e_j(F_j^* - F_j - \Pi_j)_t + \sum_{j=1}^{J} \Delta e_{jt} Z_{jt} + \Delta B_{ot}$$

The decision rule for foreign-currency borrowing which emerges is:

$$F_{jt} = a_0 + a_1 \Delta A_j - a_2 DEP_j \tag{10}$$

which has the following restrictions, $a_0 = 0$, for a one-period model, and

$$a_1 = a_2$$
$$a_1 = a_2 = 1$$

This decision rule for foreign borrowing is a behavioural relationship, not an identity.

---

[16]Unfortunately in the present study, the separability assumption (i.e. bilateral relations) cannot be directly tested due to a lack of individual company data.

The desired net contribution in home currency is $V_j'^d = \hat{e}_j(F_j^* - F_j - \hat{\Pi}_j)$, that is, a function of (as this is behavioural relationship) the expected exchange-rate times the desired less actual foreign borrowing less expected earnings. In other words, the $V_j'^d$ is the residual form of financing foreign currency denominated assets.

Now, since in fact $F_j = F_j^*$, as actual foreign borrowing will normally adjust rapidly to the desired level, then

$$V_i'^d = \hat{e}_j(F_j^* - F_j) - \hat{e}_j\Pi_j = -\hat{e}_j\Pi_j$$

and

$$V_{jt}' = e_{jt}(F_j^* - F_j) - e_{jt}\Pi_{jt} = -e_{jt}\Pi_{jt}.$$

The decision rule for home-currency financing is then

$$V_{jt}' = b_0 + b_1\Delta A_j - b_2 DEP_j - b_3 F_j - b_4\Pi_j \qquad (11)$$

with the restrictions

$$b_0 = 0$$
$$b_1 = b_2 = b_3 = b_4 = 1$$

Substituting equation (10) and (11) yields

$$V_{jt}' = (b_0 - b_3 a_0) + (b_1 - b_3 a_1)\Delta A_j - (b_2 - a_2 b_3)DEP_j - b_4\Pi_j)$$
$$(12)$$

$$= b_0' + b_1'\Delta A_j - b_2' DEP_j - b_4\Pi_j$$

where

$$b_0' = b_1' = b_2' = 0 \text{ and } b_4 = 1.$$

In this simple-risk model, the firm borrows in each currency up to the point where foreign borrowings as a positive function of asset changes (taken to be the total financing requirements of the affiliate) are not offset by depreciation allowances (the largest source of internal cash flow derived from previous investment). It has been assumed that, given the rapid adjustment of actual financing to the equilibrium levels, the flows of foreign-currency financing are functions of changes in the level of foreign assets.

It might be recalled that as DEP_i and A_j are determined by the process of maximizing the market value of the firm, they are pre-determined with respect to the financing decision.

In this simplified version, foreign-currency financing is related, in part, to changes in total assets in the ith currency. As observed on pp. 15–18, there may be arguments in favour of concentrating on current-asset changes only. It is generally understood that investment in fixed assets abroad (property, plant and equipment) is relatively free of exchange risk, since it is anticipated that any change in the exchange rate will be offset without significant lag – or with a lag short enough to be unimportant to the ordinary corporate investor – by an opposite change in the price of the real assets. This is self-evident for internationally-traded goods where the law of one price applies. It is not so clear in producing assets, unless the economy adjusts to the exchange-rate change homogeneously. Plant and equipment would presumably adjust in value to exchange depreciation by increases in prices which would be most complete in import-competing industry (where the country was a price-taker), next in export industry, and lastly in purely domestic lines. These distinctions notwithstanding, the accounting rule generally is to assume that real assets abroad are not 'exposed' to exchange risk, on the ground that the price of the assets will change oppositely to the exchange rate and in proportion – the assumption of homogeneity in effect. Only current assets and all liabilities fixed in money are exposed to risk to the extent that 'conversion' of fixed assets does not take place and where share-holders do not look beyond standard accounting conventions. From the point of view of economic theory, there is no *a priori* reason to exclude fixed assets, although an exclusive focus by management on current assets only at risk, might denote an extreme stage of 'exchange illusion'.

Going back to p. 85, it was assumed that bilateral exchange rate expectations were independent of one another such that cov $e_j e_j = 0$. This was based on the notion presented on pp. 72–3, that, in the short-run planning horizon of non-financial firms and given their relative lack of sophistication in currency matters, interest parity and purchasing-power parity have not usually been applied to the financing of foreign assets by most non-financial companies. If this assumption were not made then,

$$\pounds = \sum_j \text{var } e_j \Pi_j^2 = 2\sum_{j'} \sum_j \text{cov } e_{j'}e_j\Pi_{j'}\Pi_j + \ldots$$

and

$$\frac{\partial \pounds}{\partial F_j} = 2 \text{ var } e_j(\Delta A_j - DEP_j - F_j)$$

$$+ 2 \sum_i \sum_j \text{cov } e_{j'}e_j(\Delta A_{j'} - DEP_{j'} - F_{j'})$$

so that

$$F_j = (\Delta A_j - DEP_j) + \sum_i \sum_j \frac{\text{cov } e_{j'}e_j}{\text{var } e_j}(\Delta A_j - DEP_j - F_j)$$

$$F_j = F_j^* + \sum_j \beta_{j'j}(F_j^* - F_{j'})$$

where F_j^* is the desired amount of borrowing in the ith currency.

In Stevens' formulation (see Chapter IV), it was assumed that $\beta_{j'j} = 0, j' \neq j$. If individual company data were available, then the above relationship for foreign-currency financing could be tested and some evidence for treating the exchange rate as a random variable might be forthcoming. It should be noted that the desired value of foreign-currency borrowing on p. 87 is a behavioural relationship, not an identity. F^* is a positive function of asset changes and a negative function of depreciation provisions, representing the major source of internal funds. On the other hand, the identity for foreign borrowing would be derived directly from equation (3) as equal to assets less internal funds and net home-country financing.

An Aggregative Time-series Model

We are now ready to investigate the causal relationships between changes in foreign assets and the alternative means for their financing. A model is constructed, simple enough to be estimated, using time-series data, that captures the essential relationships and which breaks down the asset and liability side of the accounting identity in equation (3) into five variables, summing over the i currencies, j countries and k enterprises:

$$\sum_i \sum_j \sum_k e_i \Delta A_{ijk} = \sum_i \sum_j \sum_k V'_{ijk} + \sum_i \sum_j \sum_k e_i (F_{ijk} + N_{ijk}) + u_{ok}$$
(3)

where ΔA_{ijk} is changes in total assets;

         V'_{ijk} is net capital outflow in home currency, (or $V_{ijk} - DP_{ijk}$, gross outflows less dividends)

         F_{ijk} is foreign currency financing;

         N_{ijk} is cash flow of the affiliate (or $\Pi_{ijk} + DEP_{ijk}$);

and u is a residual flow of liabilities, small in magnitude and here hypothesized to be essentially random, made up of changes in certain commercial claims and bank loans to foreign affiliates.

Of the five variables, two are exogenous, ΔA and N, two are endogenous, V' and F, and one is a random residual, u. We will look at each of these variables in turn.

The change in assets of each affiliate is determined by the process of maximization of the value of the firm which is assumed in the present theory. Our focus is on how these asset changes are financed. Investment in various assets in different countries are determined by relative return criteria — the decision to invest in fixed assets, inventory, or receivables is principally dictated by expected profits, sales and competitive considerations. In the present model, it is assumed that the investment decision is already made.

There are several reasons for this choice. One is that it is in the nature of a non-financial company, depending on its industry, competition and organization, to hold assets in certain proportions, the margins of which cannot be substantially changed in the short run. A firm needs working capital to pay its creditors, wages, taxes; it must hold inventory for sales; it usually will need to grant credit to promote sales; it must invest in fixed assets to assure future sales and profitability. Investment in assets will largely be determined by the return and risk criteria associated with each asset — this is the essence of the portfolio approach. In addition, substantial disaggregation is required between industries as the structure of the asset side of the balance sheet will be primarily determined by business (operations) variables and only marginally by financial variables.

Therefore, the notion that a multinational enterprise, or indeed that any firm, is a corporate body concentrating large quantities of funds in its financial management who may then shift and employ these funds as virtually freely available financial assets at will, does not appear to correspond to reality. The flows of resources in any company are primarily devoted to the physical functions of production (either of goods or services), sales and investment in which the company is engaged, and unattached financial assets are not a normal feature of these companies.[17] It is therefore assumed that a non-financial company has a very small percentage of its total assets invested in liquid or financial assets.[18]

We are primarily concerned with the financing of total assets by a company in a particular currency. However, asset changes, although outside the scope of this study, cannot be totally disregarded. At the margin, and especially in times of currency disorders or political unrest, they can be significant. Fund flows are themselves a derivative of balance-sheet items, i.e. they are transfers of assets and liabilities, or payments of income on these. Thus, an alteration in fund flows made for the purpose of accommodating a currency change cannot be without an effect on the balance-sheet items. Indeed, there is

---

[17] See Hymer, op. cit., Chapter Five.
[18] If the data were available, it would be interesting to test the model on companies according to the proportion of financial assets out of total assets.

a complementarity between the two; in many cases a change in a fund flow cannot be initiated without an appropriate preliminary redeployment of the balance-sheet items. This situation may pertain, in particular, to short-term assets and liabilities.

With the possible exception of liquid assets, the changes in total assets in a particular affiliate will be governed by commercial, rather than financial considerations. The assumption, therefore, of a given amount of assets to be financed appears to be reasonable. Where this is not the case, the implication in terms of the present theory is that the risk perceptions are of such a significant magnitude that they cannot be minimized through the 'normal' deployment of the liability side of the balance sheet in different currencies so as to neutralize the risk factor in these particular foreign assets.

The cash flow variable, N, is composed of net profits after local tax, Π, and of provisions for depreciation, DEP. These internal sources of finance are exogenous, being clearly determined by factors beyond the original control of financial management. The earnings of a company are ultimately decided by the level of demand in the overall economy for its products, and by the success of the marketing division of the company in exploiting this potential. The company's earnings would at the same time reflect the balance between revenue from sales, and the cost of production and of other items of expenditure outside the control of financial management (except the cost of debt); the latter are conditional upon the economic organization of the production processes – the maintenance of technological standards and of maximum economy in the use of labour and materials, and the best possible exploitation of research results, etc. The earnings which go into cash flow are in themselves net of taxation, the latter being determined by national and local authorities beyond the control of company financial services.[19] Similarly, depreciation provisions are contingent upon the level of earnings on the one hand, and the level of investment deemed suitable on the other; the latter is determined, again, by

[19] See, for example, W. A. P. Manser, *The Financial Role of Multinational Enterprise*, London: Cassell, 1973, Chapter 5.

future prospects for production and marketing determined by the company's management as a whole. The calculation of these provisions will be made according to legal and professional criteria outside the discretion of the firm.

Two endogenous variables remain to be explained: V' and F. The net contribution of home-currency funds to finance foreign assets, V', will, according to the risk-reduction hypothesis outlined above, be positively related to asset changes and a negative function of the alternative sources of funds, F and N, or foreign-generated funds in the form of foreign currency borrowing and internal cash flow. This formulation corresponds to the notion, based on the separability theorem, that home-currency funds are essentially used as a residual source of finance.

This specification would explain the large amount of initial parent-company financing made when an affiliate is first established or acquired. The change in assets, in that case, would be substantial whereas there would be almost no profits from which dividends could be paid out to the parent company. At the same time, the other and major internal source of funds, depreciation allowances, would be small as there would be little or no past investment. Foreign borrowing, particularly without a parent guarantee, will be limited by the reputation and credit standing of the affiliate to borrow in its own name, even on an overdraft or trade-credit basis. On the other hand, this formulation would account for the normally observed pattern of a very small or, usually, negative net parent-company contribution over time. In this latter case, when profits were being generated, it would be expected that repatriated profits, DP, would be greater than any gross capital contribution by the parent company, V.

Recalling that $V' = V - DP$, or the net parent-company contribution equals gross capital outflows minus dividends, the higher the dividends due to higher profits — so long as the change in assets is not substantial (in which case, a greater profit retention would be anticipated) — the lower the value of V' will be for any value of V.

Only in situations where, due to marketing or technological changes, asset accumulation is substantial or where losses are made, would the parent company be deemed to be a significant source of asset financing. With low or negative earnings, the internal cash flow will be inadequate to finance asset changes for a given level of depreciation provisions and without a consistent and positive earnings' record, lenders will not be ready to advance loans nor suppliers to make credit available.

By re-arranging equation (3) to separate out the two components of V', V and DP, it can be readily observed from the identity itself that the greater the alternative sources of finance – cash flow and foreign-currency funds – the lower the need for gross parent-company contributions, for a given level of asset changes:

$$\sum_i \sum_j e_i \Delta A_{ij} = \sum_i \sum_j [e_i(\Pi_{ij} + DEP_{ij}) - DP_{ij}]$$

$$+ \sum_i \sum_j e_i F_{ij} + \sum_i \sum_j V_{ij} + u$$

where the first term on the right-hand side is the net internal sources of funds.

Thus far, it has been assumed implicitly that the model operates in time simultaneously with current sources of funds as functions of investment in current assets and current provisions for depreciation charges. It may be, in fact, that currency flows in the current period are determined by profits resulting from past investments and depreciation on past assets, depending on the previous earnings' record of the affiliate, and may result in present residual sources of funds being related to previous asset and financial decisions. As the model developed here is one of comparative statics, however, there is no theoretical justification for the insertion of lagged variables.

The remaining variable, foreign-currency borrowing, F, will be a positive function of asset changes (perhaps, in particular, to current-asset changes) and a negative function of depreciation provisions. Higher depreciation allowances – as the major component of cash flow – by increasing the internal funds available to the affiliate will decrease the recourse to local borrowing to finance a given amount of asset acquisitions. As debts are also being repaid as new loans are undertaken, the greater the internal cash flow due to higher depreciation provisions, the more likely the affiliate will be to retire the outstanding debt which has a higher cost than internal funds.

Foreign-currency funds are available to an affiliate in many different forms. Foreign-currency funds could be provided indirectly by the parent company through another foreign affiliate or financial holding company, or through local bank loans including overdraft facilities, suppliers' credits or even bond and equity issues. Much of the business literature is concerned with these various alternatives. Third-country financing by other foreign affiliates — pooling excess funds within the MNE — represents, in theory, a large potential instrument for achieving an optimal pattern for financing operations, but the complexity in reality, both institutional and administrative, greatly limits their use.[20] Bond issues and equity issues are usually made directly by parent companies, for instance, on the Eurobond markets where a lower coupon can be obtained. Equity issues by affiliates are rare as parent companies are usually reluctant to dilute their control for financial reasons.

Another variable that might be significant in determining the relative amounts of home-currency and foreign-currency financing is time. It is plausible to believe that home-currency financing as a proportion of total sources of funds to finance foreign assets will decline over time relative to foreign-currency sources for two reasons. One is that initially the foreign affiliate is relatively unknown to local suppliers and financial institutions, and so will only be able to depend heavily on local credit once its profitability record is established. Within the same framework, it is likely that over time, internal cash flow will increase as rising stocks of investment generate higher sales and so higher earnings and depreciation allowances. Secondly, there is the empirically observed

[20] See Robbins and Stobaugh, 1973, op. cit., page 63.

phenomenon of greater improvements and integration of local and international capital markets since the Second World War — a decreasing amount of market segmentation — and an increasing awareness on the part of the firm of these sources.

VII EMPIRICAL RESULTS

In this chapter the theoretical model of risk reduction in the financing of foreign assets, related to the changes in foreign-currency assets and cash flows of foreign affiliates, is tested against aggregated time-series data for a large sample of US-based manufacturing companies operating in seven European countries and Canada. Both the statistical tests run using a simple, OLS model and the graphical presentations of the data tend to support the theory presented above. On the other hand, the alternative portfolio models tested showed little statistical significance with respect to the flows financing foreign direct investment. During the period 1966–76, a time of upheaval in the international monetary system (and in the world economy) when exchange rate expectations were generally credited with determining the direction and magnitude of capital flows, it would appear that most US-based manufacturing MNEs were subject to 'exchange illusion' in the choice of currencies for financing their foreign-asset acquisitions. Only towards the end of that period did some companies operating in a few countries seem to recognize the costs in treating foreign-currency assets as riskier per se than US-dollar denominated assets. Unfortunately, a lack of more current data prevents us from determining whether the increased weakness of the dollar in more recent years has hastened the decline of 'exchange illusion' on the part of American direct investors.[1]

In analysing the determinants of the financial decisions of

---

[1] It might be, however, that in this subsequent period, the application of FASB 8 to the financial statements of US-based companies, requiring the translation of unrealized foreign-exchange losses into the consolidated financial statements, could reinforce the view that foreign currency assets are inherently riskier in terms of home-currency balance sheets.

US direct investors in eight OECD countries from 1966 to 1976[2] it is necessary to situate these phenomena in a broader economic context. The theory developed in the previous chapter does not pretend to explain 100 per cent of the variation in financial flows to foreign affiliates. Instead, it attempts to isolate the major determinants which are within the realm of management perception and control. But it cannot be ignored that other factors outside the discretion of the parent companies may have a significant influence on the financial decisions of firms. These factors can be loosely grouped into three categories: institutional, governmental, and macro-economic, and are discussed in relation to the individual country results presented below. This caveat is important because the scope of the present study is limited to testing whether the existence of market segmentation due to 'exchange illusion' of non-financial companies with foreign operations is more significant in determining the capital flows financing foreign-asset acquisitions than more traditional portfolio models which explain such flows as a function of exchange-rate changes and interest-rate differentials.

In this chapter, the nature of the data and their relation to the theoretical constructs are first discussed. Then, the aggregate results are presented and assessed. The economic context, in which the model is tested, is described and a summary of the country results is presented. The individual country results are set out using the model developed here, and comparing them with alternative, portfolio models run on the same data.

Characteristics of the Data

The theoretical models are tested against annual sources and uses of funds (i.e. balance-sheet changes) reported

---

[2] Although only seven destinations of US direct investment are tested since Belgium and Luxembourg have maintained a strict parity between their two currencies within the Belgium–Luxembourg Economic Union during and since the observation period.

by majority-owned affiliates of US parent companies in eight countries, the Belgium-Luxembourg Economic Union (BLEU), Canada, France, Germany, Italy, Netherlands and the UK from 1966 to 1976. The sample consists of those affiliates reporting the required information for all eleven years.

The sample contains 178 American parent companies in manufacturing with 3300 foreign affiliates worldwide which accounted for 16 per cent of the total number of majority-owned affiliates in the 1966 Department of Commerce benchmark survey. However, the sample accounted for 59 per cent of the dollar value of American direct investment in Europe in that year. The data were kindly furnished through an agreement with the Bureau of Economic Analysis of the US Department of Commerce which stipulated the use of aggregated results only. Although the use of more disaggregated data would have been preferable, confidentiality safeguards requiring a large number of suppressed items did not make this feasible. The sample is none the less reasonably homogeneous, consisting of large, established companies engaged mainly in technology or marketing intensive manufacturing.

The data for the individual host countries are being used for the first time in this study[3] and represent a marked improvement over the statistics available for testing in earlier studies. Comparing the data to those used by Stevens in his earlier, risk-reduction model can be instructive.[4] Stevens also used data compiled by the US Department of Commerce for US direct investment in manufacturing. Yet, although the best available at the time, 1957–65, they suffer from at least five weaknesses not found in the present study. First, the data on sources and uses of funds employed by Stevens were based on voluntary, annual surveys conducted by the Commerce Department. Many affiliates only reported sporadically so that their inclusion makes the series inconsistent as the

---

[3] Although the aggregated data without the individual country breakdowns (except for Canada and the UK) for the years 1966–76 were recently published in I. M. Mantel, 'Sources and Uses of Funds of Majority-owned Foreign Affiliates of U.S. Companies, 1973–76', *Bureau of Economic Analysis Staff Paper*, May 1979.

[4] Stevens, in Machlup, Salant, and Tarshis, 1972, op. cit.

group of underlying, reporting firms can vary. The present sample consists of affiliates reporting consecutively for all eleven years, 1966–76. Secondly, his data included replies by minority-owned, foreign affiliates. In such cases, the US parent company may not be in a position to control the financial operations so that it would not be expected that the behaviour of these affiliates would conform to the model developed. The present study includes only majority-owned, foreign affiliates. Thirdly, the survey data used by Stevens was expanded to universe estimates which has two distinct disadvantages: the introduction of estimating errors and the inclusion of a heterogeneous range of firm sizes and characteristics. Fourthly, Stevens' data refer to direct investment worldwide. Yet it would be expected that the determinants of financial behaviour vary between countries with relatively sophisticated capital markets and those without an indigenous financial infrastructure, not to mention differences in governmental factors. Lastly, there is the fact that Stevens' data only contain nine observation points with the inherent problem of simultaneity bias. The sample used in the present study contains eleven observation periods, which is still econometrically weak, although, with individual tests for seven currency areas, the aggregated results are reinforced by tests run over an additional seventy-seven observation points.

The data used in this study are not perfect proxies for the variables postulated in the theoretical models. For one thing, the data are annual with only eleven observation periods. Short-term changes and window dressing for year-end results cannot be analysed. For this reason, the strength of the model should be judged by the signs and significance of the t-ratios rather than by the correlation coefficients. In other words, given the limited number of observations, the results may be interpreted as lending support for the risk-reduction hypothesis, but should be employed with caution for predictive purposes.

Borrowing in foreign currencies, F, corresponds to the change in liabilities and net worth to foreigners. The latter is an imperfect measure as it contains no doubt some borrowings in dollars. The extent of these transactions is probably limited as the vast bulk of Eurodollar borrowings are made directly by US parent companies and only exceptionally by. foreign affiliates themselves. It is further assumed that the change in the value of assets denominated in foreign currencies is proportional to the change in the value of total assets (ΔA).

It is also possible that some of the gross parent-company contribution, V, could be made in foreign currency, although, in practice, this too is quite exceptional, even when loans extended by other US residents to foreign affiliates are included as in the case of the present data (i.e. V represents all dollar financing by US residents including the parent company and third parties).

The data for the explanatory variables in the alternative portfolio models were all derived from various issues of OECD Main Economic Indicators. Nominal interest-rate differentials, INT, are the differences in annual averages of end-of-month three-month Treasury-bill rates or closest equivalent (see Fig. 6). Spot exchange rates, EX, are the annual average of daily spot rates (see Table 5). Forward exchange rates, using the annual average of end-of-month forward exchange rates, are combined with INT and EX to derive the annual, average, covered interest-rate differentials, $COINT$.

Given the nature of the sample, the results of testing the theory cannot claim universal significance, but are limited in time and space. The model applies only to US companies in manufacturing. It can be inferred but not tested that the results would apply to direct investors of different home countries and in other industries. It may be posited that European parent companies would have less exchange illusion than US direct investors so that somewhat different results would be expected.[5]

The model is tested for the financing of assets in eight OECD member countries with relatively developed capital markets and banking institutions, stable political climates and

[5] See pp. 73–4.

where companies have been 'relatively' free of administrative and exchange controls to borrow locally, repatriate dividends, etc. The model may not apply to those non-OECD countries where institutional constraints or administrative procedures or political considerations constitute the main determinants of fund flows to finance assets.

The model has only been tested over a limited period of time, from 1966 to 1976. As noted above, this period was significant for the currency upheavals and modification in international monetary relations. It is not clear that the model would predict future currency-financing patterns, particularly as the time trend may be in the process of considerably reducing the 'exchange illusion' of US direct investors, thereby leading to capital flows in some cases which contribute to the recent depreciation of the dollar.

The Empirical Models Tested

Several slight variations of the theoretical model are tested using OLS regression techniques. The same symbols are used here as in the theoretical model and in the accounting identity on p. 62 (see the list on pp. 106–7). It is assumed that the managers of the firm are attempting to maximize the present value of the firm in terms of home-country currency. They then seek, in their bilateral relationships with foreign affiliates, to minimize the risk of losses due to exchange-rate changes in each of the jth currencies. If all hedging against such changes is done by using foreign-currency borrowing or funds generated abroad, then equation (10) from p. 87 is posited for borrowing by affiliates in foreign currencies:

$$F_{jt} = a_0 + a_1 \Delta A_j - a_2 DEP_j + u_0 \qquad (10)$$

Following from the discussion on pp. 15–18, in which it is contended that, due to standard accounting conventions, current assets in particular are exposed to exchange risk, a variation is tested using changes in current assets, ΔCA, instead of total asset changes, ΔA. In some countries, such as Canada and Germany, where the major source of foreign borrowing is supplier credits for the purchase of inventory, changes in inventory as the major portion of current-assets changes are highly significant.

From equation (11) on p. 88, the decision rule for net-home-currency financing of foreign assets can be expressed as:

$$V'_{jt} = b_0 + b_1 \Delta A_j - b_2 DEP_j - b_3 F_j - b_4 \Pi_j + u_1. \quad (11)$$

Furthermore, as $N = \Pi + DEP$, a variation of the above, can be written as:

$$V'_{jt} = b'_0 + b'_1 \Delta A_j - b'_2 N_j - b'_3 F_j + u'_1 \quad (11')$$

In addition, some *ad hoc* tests involving the inclusion of a time trend are also applied in some cases to make the simple causal model developed here more realistic by examining the possibility of learning over time.

As stated on p. 100, the main purpose of the empirical tests, besides supporting the risk-reduction hypothesis, is to compare the significance of the results, implying substantial capital-market segmentation, with more traditional, portfolio-adjustment models in which capital flows are a function of interest-rate differentials and exchange-rate expectations. As observed in Chapter IV above, empirical specifications of portfolio models are fraught with difficulties, especially in finding a proxy for exchange-rate expectations and for a wealth variable. Two different portfolio models of varying sophistication are tested below. A very simple *post hoc* model of the type used by Branson (see p. 32) is specified in which the wealth term is dropped and in which exchange rate changes from $t - 1$ to t are used with:

$$V' = \alpha_0 + \alpha_1(e_{jt-1} - e_{jt}) + \alpha_2(i_{ot} - i_{jt}) \quad (13)$$

$$F = \beta_0 + \beta_1(e_{jt-1} - e_{jt}) + \beta_2(i_{ot} - i_{jt}) \quad (14)$$

This portfolio model hypothesizes that net capital flows from the home country and foreign borrowing are functions of exchange rate changes $(e_{jt-1} - e_{jt})$ and of interest-rate differentials $(i_{jt} - i_{ot})$. A somewhat more sophisticated portfolio-adjustment model involves using the forward exchange rate as a proxy for exchange-rate expectations. This model would stipulate that net capital flows to finance foreign investment are a function of the covered interest-rate differentials, *COINT*, so that a MNE can fully offset exchange risk through forward swaps (hedging) and raise funds at the lowest nominal cost (similar to Tsiang's designation that traders fully hedge their currency exposure − see p. 27), using the formulation:

$$V' = \alpha_0' + \alpha_1' COINT + \epsilon_0' \qquad (15)$$

and
$$F = \beta_0' + \beta_1' COINT + \epsilon_1' \qquad (16)$$

The risk-reduction theory of foreign finance, as expressed in the empirical model, is broadly supported by the data both at the aggregate and individual national levels with most coefficients having the expected sign and level of significance as expressed by the *t*-ratio. The restrictions on the co-efficients implied by the theory appear to hold in most cases or, at least, can be readily explained. On the other hand, the portfolio models yield poor results in almost all cases. It should be stressed that, given the simplicity of the risk reduction model, the results are, econometrically-speaking, very significant compared to the portfolio models. By employing more powerful techniques, it may be possible to increase the statistical significance of the portfolio-adjustment interpretations. It is the very fact that the model developed here yields such significant results using a simple OLS model, however, that permits us to reject an equally simple portfolio-adjustment explanation of capital flows financing foreign direct investment. To begin with, the data were grouped together for all seven currency areas (i.e. the eight countries) in the sample to observe the overall trends. After a discussion of the main results, a summary of the individual country results is presented followed by a brief description of the results of each country.

For an interpretation of the empirical results, the following list is used:

V   is the gross capital flow in home-country currency to the foreign affiliate;

V' is the net capital flow in home-country currency, which is equal to V less DP, distributed profits;

N is the internal cash flow of the affiliate, consisting of Π plus DEP;

DP is distributed profits or dividends paid to the parent company by the foreign affiliate;

Π is the profits of the foreign affiliate in terms of home currency;

DEP is depreciation provisions of the foreign affiliate;

F is financing in foreign currency, mostly in that of the host country, but including contributions by other foreign affiliates;

ΔA is changes in total assets invested in the foreign affiliate.

PPE is property, plant and equipment expenditure by the foreign affiliate or investment in fixed assets;

ΔCA is the change in current assets of the foreign affiliate, or $\Delta A - PPE$;

$TIME$ is a time-trend variable;

EX is the change in the annual, average spot rate of the foreign currency in terms of the US dollar;

INT is the nominal interest-rate differential, using the annual average of end-of-month three-month Treasury-bill rates or equivalent, with the foreign rate minus the US rate;

$COINT$ is the annual average covered interest differential from the point of view of the foreign affiliate defined as

$$\left[\frac{\text{forward rate}}{EX} \right]^4 \times 100 - 100 + INT.$$

Aggregated Results

Before interpreting the regression results, it may be useful to observe and to analyse the trends shown in Figs. 3–5.

In Fig. 3, the total assets to be financed in all eight sample countries together are displayed with the three basic sources of funds analysed in the present study — internal cash flow,

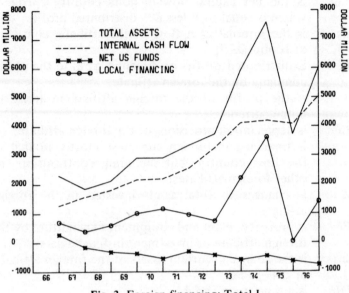

Fig. 3 Foreign financing: Total I

N, net US funds, V' and foreign funds, F. The residual (other sources of funds), while at times important, is not shown or analysed as it was not possible to distinguish their origin. It is however suspected that other sources are probably mostly derived from internal sources due to an under-reporting of declared profits in some cases.

Some interesting features emerge. Internal funds display a fairly steady growth rate of about 17.5 per cent per year, generated by net profits and depreciation allowances. Over the entire sample period, 1966–76, internal funds accounted for an average of 76.0 per cent of all sources of foreign asset financing. This result accords with our expectations that internal sources would predominate. Furthermore, most of the companies in the sample had some recent affiliates established in the early 1960s in Europe so that it would be expected that internal funds cover a low percentage of asset changes in the beginning of the observation period. This expectation is borne out. Internal cash flow accounted for only 55.4 per cent of total financing in 1966 (against an average 76.0 per cent for the whole period), but rose to 84.0 per cent by 1976. Only in two years, 1973 and 1974, did this rising trend of internal funds fall back significantly. In 1973, internal funds declined to 69.4 per cent of total sources, and in 1974 they declined further to 55.2 per cent, although still increasing in absolute terms. Over the sample period, both profits and depreciation provisions consistently accounted for about one-half of internal funds (with depreciation averaging 51.2 per cent).

Foreign source funds, on the other hand, display a certain volatility over the sample period although they tend to be highly correlated with asset changes. It would appear, in fact, that foreign-financing sources are used to make up the difference where internal funds are inadequate to finance total-asset changes, such as at early stages of new operations or when assets are growing very rapidly. This is borne out by the data. On average, foreign financing accounted for 30.2 per cent of total sources of funds. But in 1966, when many affiliates were still in their early stages, foreign funds accounted for 30.3 per cent. This percentage had fallen to 23.5 per cent by 1976. The rather high average figure of 30.2 per cent is caused by three exceptional years, 1970, 1973, and 1974, noted above where internal funds were unable to cover the financing of rapid asset accumulation. Foreign funds rose to 37.4 per cent of total sources in 1973 and to 47.7 per cent in 1974.

Looking now at the graph of foreign funds only (Fig. 4), which disaggregates foreign sources into its three respective components: affiliate funds, banking sources and non-banking sources (i.e. mainly suppliers' credits). Affiliate funds, whether provided by other producing affiliates or financial holding companies, were a relatively minor, although stable, source of foreign funds. This is despite the potential use of such funds – through global corporate pooling – to minimize the cost of debt. Institutional factors as well as the sheer complexity of such operations, not least from an accounting point of view and in terms of affiliate management incentives, are probably responsible. On average, affiliate funds accounted for 8.7 per cent of foreign funds from 1966 to 1976.

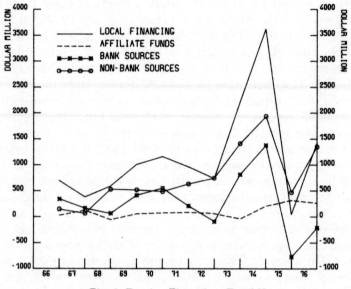

Fig. 4 Foreign Financing: Total II

One interesting feature of affiliate funds that is in accordance with our expectations concerns the learning process over time in which financial management gains experience in dealing with administrative complexities. From 1966 to 1973, in the period before most currencies began substantial floating, affiliate funds accounted for only 4.2 per cent of foreign funds. From 1974 to 1976, a more sophisticated financial management used affiliate funds to account for 15.5 per cent of foreign-source funds.

Both local banking funds and suppliers' credits were important as sources of foreign-currency funds. Suppliers' credits accounted for 64.5 per cent of these sources and banking funds accounted for 22 per cent of this sub-total. During the earlier part of the observation period, from 1966 to 1970, however, banking funds were relatively more important than later on, accounting for 39.8 per cent of foreign funds, against 45.2 per cent for suppliers' credits. Suppliers' credits are tied to purchases of inventory so that, before the large inflationary rises in inventory prices starting in the early

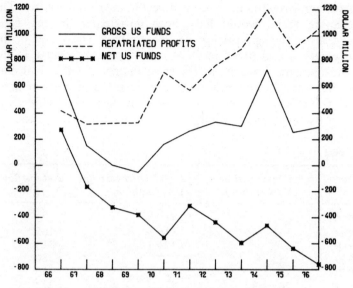

Fig. 5 Foreign financing: Total III

1970s, their use is more limited. Any additional finance for working capital needs would come from local banks or from foreign branches of American banks. Bank borrowing may have been used in any case initially for those affiliates of relatively recent origin wishing to establish their 'credit image' with local bankers in view of possible, future borrowing needs.

Turning now to US-dollar financing in Fig 5, the results, while in accordance with our expectations, appear surprising to those observers anticipating a more versatile use of US funds to finance foreign assets. A slightly declining trend in the use of dollar sources is clear over the whole observation period. We would expect US funds to be relatively important during earlier stages of an affiliate's life before cash flow can be generated and local funds obtained. In 1966, gross US funds accounted for 30.1 per cent of total sources and even net US funds (i.e. less repatriated earnings) were 11.9 per cent of total sources.

The US mandatory programme to limit dollar financing

of foreign investment is not noticeable in the net figures. The declining trend would have been anticipated in any case. Even after the application of the controls was eased in the early 1970s and lifted in 1974, no observable change in the trend appears. Looking at the gross figures in Table 1, it may be that the US controls may have resulted in a lower gross dollar outflow in 1968 and 1969 in particular which was offset by lower than average dividends in those two years.

Table 1

Year	Gross outflow V ($ million)	Repatriated earnings DP ($ million)	Net outflow V' ($ million)
1966	692	419	273
1967	151	316	−165
1968	1	324	−323
1969	−53	327	−380
1970	162	717	−555
1971	265	577	−312
1972	333	770	−437
1973	300	896	−506
1974	737	1199	−462
1975	256	895	−639
1976	295	1056	−761

Over the entire observation period, 1966–76, net US funds accounted for −10.3 per cent of total sources. That is, the net contribution of dollar financing was in fact negative. As noted above, in 1966, net dollar financing was a positive 11.9 per cent of total sources. This percentage steadily declined to −13 per cent in 1976. In absolute terms, from 1966 to 1976 in the eight sample countries, American sources contributed $3.1 billion to foreign affiliates, but, on the other hand, they received $7.5 billion in dividends.

Other, unspecified sources of funds, probably attributable for the most part to an under reporting of profits – hence internal sources – accounted for an average of 4.1 per cent of total sources over the observation period, ranging from 2.5 per cent in 1966 to 5.2 per cent in 1976.

The results of the regression tests run on the explanatory

variables tend to confirm the above graphical analysis, and are presented below in two tables showing the determinants of foreign financing and of net home-currency financing respectively.[6]

Concerning the equations for foreign-currency financing, the coefficients have the expected signs in both variants of the model presented in Table 2 and are significant at the 99 per cent confidence level or more in the case of three of the four coefficients.

The first equation is the basic test of the model stipulated in equation (10) in which foreign-currency financing is a positive function of total-asset changes and a negative function of depreciation provisions as the major source of internal funds. As expected, foreign-currency financing increases as a function of asset changes but is even more strongly, negatively affected by increases in depreciation. The theoretical model is supported with both of the independent variables being significant at the 99 per cent confidence level and with the model explaining 96 per cent of the variation in foreign-currency financing over the observation period.

It should be noted that in a time-series model, there is a problem in detecting the existence of serial correlation in the disturbance terms. Whereas in the other variant of the model, the Durbin–Watson statistic provides some assurance of independent residuals (with d above the upper limit of d_u), the first equation is more worrying as the DW statistic lies between the upper and lower bounds of d, which does not reject nor confirm the null hypothesis of no serial correlation among the disturbance terms. In fact, recalling the observed trend in other sources of funds, which are excluded in the regression tests, it would be surprising if some serial correlation was not detected as it is assumed that alternative financing sources would be a residual. To the extent that these alternative sources (under-reported profits and depreciation, but also possibly ω_{ij} – i.e. the separability theorem does not hold perfectly) display certain trends over time,

[6] As noted on p. 106, the limited number of observations focuses the interpretation of the results on the t-ratios.

Table 2 Foreign financing: Total*

Dependent variable	Coefficient	Independent variable	t-ratio	R^2	Adjusted R^2	DW Statistic	Standard error estimate
(1) F	224.3	Constant	1.10	0.96	0.95	1.54	226.5
	0.84	ΔA	12.21				
	-1.54	DEP	-6.77				
(2) F	464.4	Constant	1.33	0.88	0.85	1.98	383.1
	0.90	ΔCA	6.85				
	-0.42	DEP	-1.51				

*The total of foreign currency borrowing by a sample of majority-owned affiliates of US companies in eight OECD countries from 1966 to 1976.

Table 3 Net home-currency financing: Total*

Dependent variable	Coefficient	Independent variable	t-ratio	R^2	Adjusted R^2	DW Statistic	Standard error estimate
(1) V'	44.7	Constant	1.68				
	0.98	ΔA	21.36				
	-1.03	Π	-18.86	0.99	0.99	2.00	24.0
	-1.07	DEP	-17.14				
	-0.98	F	-20.00				
(2) V'	36.0	Constant	1.96				
	0.98	ΔA	22.63				
	-1.05	N	-27.34	0.99	0.99	2.00	22.6
	-0.97	F	-21.25				
(3) V'	-223.4	Constant	-1.34				
	-132.6	TIME	-3.62	0.79	0.74	1.87	141.1
	0.26	PPE	1.81				
(4) V'	12.3	Constant	0.55				
	0.95	ΔA	22.29				
	-0.98	N	-17.45	0.99	0.99	2.26	20.5
	-0.95	F	-21.67				
	-17.3	TIME	-1.59				
(5) V'	40.8	Constant	0.32	0.62	0.57	1.27	182.0
	-0.30	Π	-3.81				

*The total net amount of US dollars used to finance foreign direct investment by a sample of majority-owned affiliates of US companies in eight OECD countries from 1966 to 1976.

some serial correlation in the disturbance terms would be expected.

Turning now to the restrictions on the model, it was postulated that $a_0 = 0$, and $a_1 = a_2 = 1$. The first restriction, $a_0 = 0$, does not hold, but this would be expected. The theoretical model applies to one period and so ignores the financing flows of previous periods. In a time-series, given past foreign financing, the y-ordinate will be significantly different from zero. Only in the second equation does the second restriction hold that $a_1 = a_2 = 1$. In the first variant, the coefficient of depreciation is almost twice that of asset changes, although, using the Wald test, it can be shown that, statistically speaking, the two coefficients are not significantly different from one another. As it stands, the model indicates that increases in internal cash flow, represented by depreciation allowances, have a strong negative effect on foreign borrowing which would only be partly offset (by about one-half) by increases in assets in the jth affiliate.

Thus, depreciation allowances of foreign affiliates exert a significantly negative influence confirming the hypothesis that the greater resulting cash flow, *ceteris paribus*, will lessen the demand for locally borrowed funds and may even lead to an almost insignificant amount of foreign borrowing as occurred in one year, 1975.

The appearance of the coefficients of depreciation charges being double those of asset changes (so that $a_1 \neq a_2$) may have a simple explanation. Depreciation provisions account for the major source of cash flow along with earnings, but statistically in this regression model the depreciation term alone is carrying the negative impact of increases in internal cash flow. If, for example, depreciation were one-half of cash flow in a particular case, then in the regression test, it would serve as a statistical proxy for all internal sources, so doubling the coefficient.

The second equation also confirms an alternative version of the theory in which (following from accounting conventions described on pp. 15–18) only current asset changes are viewed as being at risk. What is interesting in the results is that both the significance levels and the correlation coefficient are weaker than in the first equation, which would indicate that MNEs view all foreign assets at risk rather than just current assets.

Concerning the five equations of determinants of net home-currency financing of foreign assets shown in Table 3, the explanatory variables carry the expected signs in all cases. The levels of significance are higher than 99 per cent in the versions directly testing the risk-reduction hypothesis.

The first and second equations represent alternative versions of the basic model as set out in equations (11) and (11′) respectively. In the second equation, the two elements of internal cash flow, depreciation provisions and profits, are combined into N, which is given by the identity of each flow on p. 62. As expected, net home-currency financing increases as a function of asset changes and is negatively affected by increases in the components of cash flow, i.e. profits and depreciation provisions. Foreign-currency borrowing also negatively affects home-currency flows. Not only do all of the explanatory variables carry the expected signs, but their statistical significance as measured by the t-statistics exceed 99 per cent in all cases. It was suggested on p. 102 that the strength of the model be judged by the t-ratios, given the small number of observations for fitting a regression line. These results confirm strongly the hypothesis. In addition, the model explains almost 100 per cent of the variation in net US dollar outflows. It would appear that the restrictions on the model indicated on p. 88 are fulfilled with the coefficients being almost equal to each other and to one, except for $b_0 = 0$. This shows that our equation based on a static, one-period model is validated by the time series.

The third regression is an *ad hoc* test of the hypothesis that home-currency funds are used when there are rapid expansions of fixed assets abroad which are viewed as possibly less prone to valuation adjustments due to currency changes. A time-trend variable is also included. The time-trend variable is, as expected, negative and highly significant, supporting the hypothesis that over time, *ceteris paribus*, internal cash flow supplemented where necessary by foreign-currency borrowing will displace the home-country contributions mainly from the parent company which become negative in net absolute terms as repatriated earnings exceed new gross-capital out-flows. The weakness of the fixed-asset change variable confirms the results that fixed assets are viewed as being as no less at risk than current assets (see p. 116). There is no evidence to support the notion that net home-currency funds finance fixed-asset expenditure in particular.[7] The fourth equation is an alternative of the second one, but including the time trend as well. The addition of the time-trend vari-able to the basic model in equation (11) has little effect on the statistical significance of the explanatory variables which con-tinue to be significant at the 99 per cent confidence level, carrying the expected signs with the restrictions on the co-efficients satisfied. Interestingly enough, in contrast to the third equation, the time trend variable itself is only signifi-cant at the 84 per cent confidence level (although it carries the expected negative sign). This could denote that the learn-ing process over time, in which MNEs lose their 'exchange illusion' as market developments and floating exchange rates alter the cost trade-offs of its acceptance as suggested on p. 73, is weaker, at least for this sample of US-based manu-facturing firms, than one might have expected on *a priori* grounds. On the other hand, the insignificance of the time trend may be due to the fact that its explanatory power is picked up statistically by the growth of the internal cash-flow variable, N. The two variables are highly correlated with an $R^2 = 0.95$.

The fifth equation is included to test the proposition on p. 88 that desired home-currency contributions are a resi-dual form of finance as a function of desired less actual foreign borrowing (which adjusts rapidly to zero) and of

[7] At least in this observation period before FASB 8 was promulgated in 1976, which required the reporting of foreign-exchange gains and losses in the consoli-dated income statement with fixed assets valued at historic exchange rates. As the dollar value of fixed assets was more stable than for current assets under this ruling, it is likely that a distinction was made in currency choices financing those respective assets. The revisions to FASB 8, expected to be introduced in Decem-ber 1981, would require firms to use the current exchange rate when translating all foreign assets into dollars, so favouring the kind of behaviour described in this study.

expected earnings. As expected, the coefficient of actual profits is negative and significant at the 99 per cent confidence level.

In interpreting the results of the empirical model, a question can be raised as to whether the high statistical significance achieved by the model simply reflects the fact that under most of the observation period, say 1966–72, these firms were operating in the context of fixed exchange rate international monetary relations (see p. 122) where the costs of accepting 'exchange-rate illusion' were low relative to the expenditure in overcoming the market imperfections which are at its source. If this were the case, then with the transition to generalized floating from 1973 onwards, a major shift in the structural parameters of the model would be expected (due to the higher cost of passively accepting 'exchange illusion' where the home currency values of foreign earnings are subject to greater uncertainty). It is therefore important to test the risk-reduction equations for stability by comparing the two sub-periods, 1966–72 and 1973–76, using the Chow test.[8]

The results of the Chow test of stability are given in Table 4 for the data aggregated over the eight countries (individual Chow-test results are discussed in the individual country section below where relevant). The test results show that the hypothesis of stability for both the foreign financing and net home-currency financing equations for the two sample periods is not rejected. This suggests, therefore, that these two equations, as estimated over the entire sample period, 1966–76, can be used to summarize those relationships. The stability of the model can also be observed graphically in Fig. 3, p. 108, where the apparent, earlier trends in the data appear to hold in the later years. So, while there is some evidence of MNEs learning over time to reduce their 'exchange illusion', say by increasing their recourse to inter-affiliate funds as observed on p. 110, the model still holds in the period of floating rates covered here. This stability is not surprising when it is recalled that, while the costs of

[8] J. Johnston, *Econometric Methods*, 1st edition, New York, McGraw Hill, 1963.

Table 4 Results of Chow test (1966–72 vs. 1973–6)

Equation	Critical F	Calculated F	Conclusion*
(10) $F_{jt} = a_0 + a_1 \Delta A_j - a_2 DEP_j + u_0$	$F_{(0.01)} = 11.4$	1.41	Cannot reject H_0
(11) $V'_{jt} = b_0 + b_1 \Delta A_j - b_2 DEP_j - b_3 F_j$ $- b_4 \Pi_j + u_1$	$F_{(0.01)} = 28.7$	10.06	Cannot reject H_0

*H_0 is the null hypothesis that the regression equations are equal for the two sample periods.

accepting 'exchange illusion' may increase under floating rates, so does the riskiness increase of investing home currency in foreign-currency assets (as measured by the variance of foreign-currency profits in terms of home currency).

Relevant Economic Background

In order to appreciate the findings on the financing of US direct investment during the period 1966–76, it would be useful to recall briefly some of the major developments – falling outside the scope of the present theory – which could also affect the size and direction of financing flows. As noted on p. 100, these factors can be loosely grouped into three categories: institutional, governmental, and macro-economic.

Institutional Factors

During the period 1966–76, at least three ongoing developments could be identified as affecting the exchange-risk perceptions of direct investors. First, the rapid development of international capital markets and the geographical spread of international banking during this period would have increased the availability and awareness of alternative sources of finance to parent companies and to their foreign affiliates. In particular, in-house corporate financial services required increasing sophistication to make efficient and profitable use of these alternative sources and of the financial advice available from competing financial institutions. To the extent that exchange illusion is a result of risk perceptions based on market segmentation, this growing sophistication on the part of direct investors should affect their financing decisions over time. This institutional characteristic may, in part, be captured in the time-trend variable in the third variant of the model.

Secondly, there were major changes in international monetary relationships during this period: the pound sterling was devalued by 14.5 per cent against the dollar in November 1967; the German Deutsche Mark was under speculative pressure and was revalued in 1969; the French franc was devalued in August 1969. The fixed exchange-rate system, dating from the Bretton Woods Agreement of July 1944, was coming under increased speculative pressure as the 1970s began. In August 1971, the gold convertibility of the dollar was suspended, leading to the Smithsonian Agreement in December 1971, where the dollar was officially devalued by raising the gold price to $38.00 an ounce. Some currencies, particularly the Deutsche Mark, Dutch guilder and Swiss franc, again came under excessive buying pressure. In February 1973, the gold price of the dollar was again raised to $42.00 an ounce and, following the revaluation and floating of the Deutsche Mark in 1972, most countries switched to floating-rate regimes. It might be noted that Canada was on a floating-rate regime during almost the entire period covered here.

Exchange markets were relatively calm in the remainder of 1973 and in 1974 and 1975. Intense speculative pressure was seen again in 1976 for appreciation of the Deutsche Mark, Swiss franc and yen, and, to a lesser extent, the guilder. These currency rates against the dollar, at average annual rates, are presented in Table 5.

Fixed exchange rates may have encouraged a form of complacency on the part of risk-averse financial managers. The system encouraged essentially one-way, risk-free speculation on currency changes as, in practice, governments were defending rates under pressure in one direction only. With more recurrent changes and especially with floating rates where currency rates can adjust in either direction, a greater degree of sophistication is required of financial management. It might be recalled that for American companies exchange illusion was encouraged by the fact that up until the beginning of the period under review, the dollar was the 'strong' currency with foreign-currency assets, by definition, subject to possible losses in dollar terms. During the course of the 1966–76 period, the dollar fell from its pinnacle and, for the first time, a real loss could be sustained by holding dollar assets or by withholding dollar liabilities to finance foreign assets. A certain inertia may be responsible for a belated and

Table 5 Nominal exchange rates
Units of national currencies against the US dollar (annual average of daily spot rates)

Year	BLEU	Canada	France	Germany	Italy	Netherlands	UK
1965	49.64	1.08	4.90	4.00	625	3.60	0.36
1966	49.83	1.08	4.91	4.00	624	3.62	0.36
1967	49.69	1.08	4.92	3.99	624	3.60	0.36
1968	49.94	1.08	4.95	4.00	623	3.62	0.42
1969	50.14	1.08	5.20	3.93	627	3.62	0.41
1970	49.66	1.04	5.53	3.65	627	3.62	0.42
1971	48.59	1.01	5.51	3.48	618	3.50	0.41
1972	44.01	1.00	4.04	3.19	583	3.21	0.40
1973	38.96	1.00	4.45	2.67	582	2.79	0.41
1974	38.96	0.98	4.81	2.59	650	2.69	0.43
1975	36.79	1.02	4.29	2.46	653	2.53	0.45
1976	38.61	0.99	4.78	2.52	832	2.64	0.56
1977	35.84	1.06	4.91	2.32	882	2.45	0.57

Source: Economic Outlook, OECD, no. 24, December 1978.

limited recognition of this exchange illusion. Once again the increasing awareness by direct investors of their exchange-rate myopia may be caught in the time trend variable.

Thirdly, it should not be ignored that, just before and during the observation period, there was a significant increase in the extent and quality of management education in the US in which international financial management was systematically studied. This expansion coincided with the need to provide informed managers for fast-expanding international operations of US companies and banks. The integration of these more numerically trained and internationally aware managers into corporate financial decision making may have also diminished the prevalence of exchange-rate illusion over time.

Governmental factors

During the observation period, parent companies and their foreign affiliates were not always free to reduce their perceived risks as desired. Due in part to the upheavals and pressures in international monetary relationships, many governments had recourse to exchange controls, banking regulations or other administrative devices to influence or regulate the use of domestic or foreign currencies. Among the most significant was the US programme of controls on foreign direct investment. This programme to limit dollar outflows to finance foreign investment was voluntary from 1965 to 1967 and mandatory from 1968 (its year of greatest intensity) until it was gradually phased out completely in 1974.

US direct investors were allotted quotas, limiting their future dollar outflows to an average, small percentage increase on the previous period to all countries in the sample (Group C) except Canada, which was exempt from the controls. An empirical study by the US Department of Commerce[9] found that, while the programme may have stimulated the acquisition of foreign current assets in excess of normally expected levels, the composition of financing flows was little altered. The results presented below bear out

[9] Berlin, op. cit.

this contention. Dollar outflows (subject to exchange illusion) in many years were below the allotted quotas and, when the controls were lifted, did not significantly increase.

Canada had no controls affecting the financial flows under consideration during this period. Belgium–Luxembourg maintained their dual-exchange market for commercial and financial operations, but as the two rates rarely diverged to any large degree, there was probably little influence on corporate financial decisions.

France had at times used exchange controls, including a two-tier exchange market in 1971 and 1972. In addition, acquisitions of French companies had to be financed in foreign (i.e. non-franc) currencies and new establishments had to be financed at least 50 per cent in foreign exchange. Periodic, but generally discretionary limitations were placed on French franc borrowing by foreign affiliates and Ministry of Finance authorization was required for franc borrowing with a parent-company guarantee.

German regulations beginning in 1972 were aimed to prevent excessive capital inflows for non-commercial purposes. Direct investors, were, in fact, little hampered by the 'bardepot' regulations for raising German funds or by limitations on increases in non-resident-controlled bank deposits. Foreign affiliates in Germany were exempt from these controls unless they were being used as financial conduits.

Direct investors in Italy were little affected by Italy's exchange controls. As in France, however, there were some occasional difficulties in obtaining local bank credit due to credit allocation and costs. In the Netherlands, there were no regulations affecting legitimate financing operations of direct investors.

The extensive exchange controls of the UK (which were abolished on 24 October 1979) had no direct application to foreign direct investors in the UK, except for occasional limitations on the availability of local bank credit to affiliates for purposes other than working capital. Similar to French administrative practices, however, 50 per cent of fixed-asset financing had to be made with foreign exchange.

Macro-economic factors

Macro-economic factors, outside the control of firms, determine the extent to which local credit is available and at what cost, the rate of inflation affecting the choice of maturities of liabilities and the rate of economic growth affecting sales, earnings and the ability to generate cash flow. In Fig. 6, the interest rate differentials between the US three-month

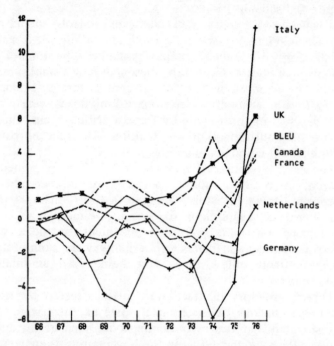

Fig. 6 Nominal interest rate differentials (national rate minus US rate; annual average of end of month figures for three-month Treasury bills or equivalent).
Source: *Main Economic Indicators*, OECD, various issues.

Treasury-bill rate and the comparable rate in the seven currencies involved are shown, as domestic economic developments are reflected in the interest rates which, according to portfolio optimization criteria, then determine the efficient allocation of capital.

One of the features of most of this period, the expansiveness of US monetary policy and ample corporate liquidity (except in 1969 and 1974), would lead to a prediction of significant net US capital outflows to finance foreign assets. This is not observed in the data for net direct investment outflows, although it is possible that US financial institutions exported substantial amounts of dollars for on-lending to the foreign affiliates of US parent companies. In this case, however, from the point of view of the MNE, it was borrowing in most cases foreign currency rather than dollars. Hence, the allegation that the over-valued dollar and easy credit policy in the US were directly responsible for the growth of American direct investment abroad would not appear to be supported (as gross dollar outflows were never a major source of financing foreign investment), except indirectly to the extent that funds, essentially denominated in foreign currencies, were more readily available from US financial institutions abroad.

Empirical Results for Individual Countries

For the eight countries in the sample (Belgium and Luxembourg as one currency area, Canada, France, Germany, Italy, the Netherlands and the UK), a summary of the statistical tests is presented. Then, the individual country results are presented and briefly described. In each case, alternative, portfolio-adjustment models (see p. 105) are also tested.

The trends and causal relationships analysed for the aggregate results are generally supported by the results in the individual host countries. Of the twenty-one equations testing the model presented in Tables 7–13, for instance, the coefficients of the explanatory variables carry the expected signs in all cases for asset changes, and in all but one case for depreciation allowances. The results are usually highly significant and appear to explain the capital flows financing foreign asset changes better than the alternative portfolio models. Concerning the foreign-financing equations, the results for France, Italy and the Netherlands are especially striking, but the results for BLEU, Canada, Germany and the UK are almost as significant and can be readily explained in the context of the theory developed above. In general, the model is more statistically significant with respect to variables explaining net US dollar financing, where results of all the equations are uniformly and highly significant, than to variables explaining foreign borrowing.

Table 6 summarizes the results, giving the sign of the coefficient and the significance level of the coefficient for each explanatory variable including the portfolio-adjustment model as indicated by the *t*-ratio. Where the same variable was used in two equations, the higher value is given (these are given separately in the country results). Likewise, correlation coefficients and the satisfaction of the *a priori* restrictions are discussed in the individual country results.

The basic model for foreign financing of US direct investment abroad i.e. equation (10), p. 87, is strongly supported by the statistical tests as well as by the graphical presentations. The correlation coefficients range from a low of 61 per cent for Germany to a high of 95 per cent for Italy. The statistical significance of the explanatory variables is strikingly high given the diversity of country situations. This is particularly true of total asset changes where the significance level is at least 99 per cent in all cases except for Germany where it was 98 per cent. The coefficients all have the expected signs. As for depreciation provisions as a proxy for cash flow, the statistical significance is at least 95 per cent for Canada, France, Italy and the Netherlands, but somewhat less significant for BLEU (0.93), the UK (0.94) and Germany (0.81). It is interesting to note that these three latter countries are those which have been among the traditional recipients of US investment so that much of the major initial investments in fixed assets had probably been made before the sample period began. In this case, depreciation may be relatively less important as a source of funds than profits generated by established operations, the affiliates may have more autonomy as they are older and larger than those in some of the other sample countries, and they may have an established 'track record' which facilitates local borrowing

Table 6 Summary of regression results using individual country data*

	ΔA	ΔCA	DEP	Π	EX	INT	COINT
Foreign financing							
BLEU	(+)0.99	(+)0.99	(−)0.93		(+)0.48	(+)0.85	(+)0.12
Canada	(+)0.99	(+)0.99	(−)0.95		(+)0.10	(−)0.03	(+)0.30
France	(+)0.99	(+)0.99	(−)0.99		(+)0.14	(+)0.97	(−)0.92
Germany	(+)0.98	(+)0.99†	(−)0.81		(+)0.83	(−)0.08	(+)0.31
Italy	(+)0.99	(+)0.99	(−)0.99		(−)0.81	(−)0.89	n.a.
Netherlands	(+)0.99	(+)0.99	(−)0.98		(+)0.31	(+)0.57	(−)0.47
UK	(+)0.99	(+)0.99	(−)0.94		(+)0.11	(−)0.08	(−)0.83
Net home currency financing							
BLEU	(+)0.99	(−)0.99	(−)0.99	(−)0.99	(−)0.09	(+)0.02	(−)0.84
Canada	(+)0.99	(−)0.99	(−)0.99	(−)0.99	(+)0.33	(−)0.40	(−)0.51
France	(+)0.99	(−)0.99	(−)0.99	(−)0.99	(−)0.31	(−)0.55	(+)0.41
Italy	(+)0.99	(−)0.99	(−)0.99	(−)0.98	(+)0.75	(+)0.50	n.a.
Netherlands	(+)0.98	(−)0.98	(−)0.95	(−)0.98	(−)0.89	(−)0.73	(+)0.23
UK	(+)0.99	(−)0.99	(−)0.99	(−)0.99	(−)0.24	(+)0.02	(−)0.15

*The statistical results presented here for the alternative models using individual national data show the signs of coefficients of the variables in parentheses and their levels of significance as indicated by the size of the *t*-ratio.

†Inventory only   n.a. Not available

from banks and suppliers, irrespective of changes in internal cash flow.

An *ad hoc* alternative of the basic model was also tested using current-asset changes only instead of total-asset changes. This was run to explore the assertion stemming from the accounting convention explained on pp. 15–18 that MNEs only view current assets at risk and so borrow abroad to hedge the currency exposure of those assets only. Compared to the basic model, there is little support for the alternative as the statistical significance and standard error estimate worsen for Canada, France, Italy, the Netherlands and the UK. Moreover, for all seven destinations, the depreciation variable becomes almost insignificant and for Germany it carries the wrong sign. For BLEU and Germany, however, the alternative using current assets only (and inventory only as the bulk of current assets for Germany), have somewhat greater explanatory power. In the case of BLEU, this is only slight (see Table 7), but for Germany, the alternative is much more robust. This may reflect tight lending conditions for bank borrowing for general financing and, hence, a reliance on suppliers' credits for inventory financing.

The basic model for home-currency financing of foreign direct investment, equation (11), p. 88, is also strongly supported. The results are summarized in Table 6. This is the model that determines the amount of net capital outflow in the balance of payments sense (and would reflect the exchange-market pressures of financing direct investment). The results are even more uniform than for the foreign-financing model. The correlation coefficient varies from 91 per cent for Italy to in excess of 95 per cent for BLEU, Canada, France, and Germany. All variables carry the expected signs and the *t*-ratios are generally significant at the 99 per cent confidence level for all explanatory variables for BLEU, Canada, France, Germany and the UK, and almost as significant for Italy and the Netherlands. The *a priori* restrictions are satisfied for BLEU, Canada, France, Germany, and Italy and, using the Wald test, are respected for the Netherlands and the UK.

In comparison, the alternative portfolio-adjustment models perform poorly in explaining the currency composition of flows financing foreign direct investment. They have only limited significance with respect to foreign-currency financing of foreign assets by US direct investors and, even then, only for France and the UK (using the covered interest differentials) and for Italy (using the *post hoc* model). In the latter three cases, they are out-performed by the risk-reduction model. For home-currency outflows, the portfolio models have some explanatory power in the case of Belgium (using the covered differentials) and for Italy and the Netherlands (using the *post hoc* model). Thus, there appears to be little support for models postulating capital flows financing foreign direct investment as a function of financial variables assumed to apply to portfolio investors. These contrasting results are all the more striking when it is recognized that the risk-reduction models are tested using simple econometric techniques against two alternatives of portfolio-adjustment models. While, no doubt, the statistical results of the portfolio models could be improved through the use of more sophisticated techniques, the economic interpretation of the results using simple regression models in both cases clearly favours the plausibility of the risk-reduction hypothesis. In addition, even the portfolio models tend to support that non-financial direct investors were subject to 'exchange illusion', although, by dividing the time period covered, it appears that, beginning in 1973 when general floating began, at least for Germany and the Netherlands, US direct investors were acquiring exchange realism as they became aware of the effects of appreciation of those currencies on dollar profits. This learning process over time in which non-financial firms may lose their exchange illusion was asserted on p. 73.

As noted on p. 124, there is almost no evidence that the US Foreign Direct Investment Program (FDIP) had an impact on the currency sources for financing US direct investment abroad, even in 1968, its year of greatest intensity. In that year, net US outflows as percentage of total sources reached their lowest point for only Italy and the Netherlands. The low point was reached in 1967 for France, 1970 for Germany, 1973 for BLEU by which time the controls had been virtually removed and 1975 for the UK after the withdrawal of the controls. What is more, for Canada, which was excluded from the controls, the financing pattern does not appear to be different from that of the other countries. For details, see Figs. 7–27.

Belgium–Luxembourg Economic Union

The results for the BLEU confirm the risk reduction theory expounded above. As shown in Figs. 7–9, internal cash flow was the major source of funds to finance asset changes with locally borrowed funds making up the bulk of the difference, particularly in 1973 and 1974. Net US funds were minimal except in 1974 when asset accumulation was extremely rapid and in 1975 when restrictive credit policies made domestic funds difficult and expensive to obtain. Over the 1966–76 period, they financed 2 per cent of total-asset acquisitions in

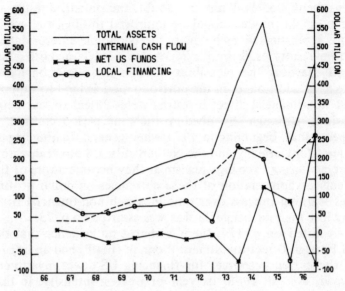

Fig. 7 Foreign financing: BLEU I

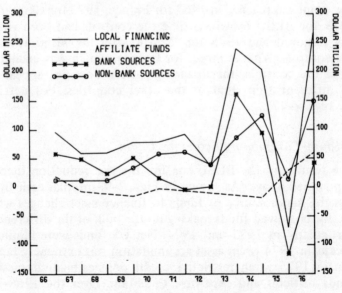

Fig. 8 Foreign Financing: BLEU II

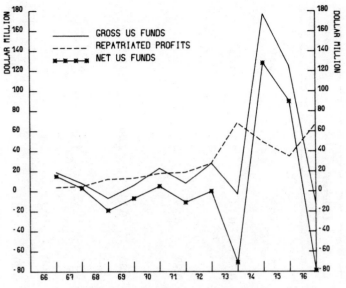

Fig. 9 Foreign financing: BLEU III

the BLEU. The regression equations display the expected signs and are highly significant.

The first equation in Table 7 fully supports the theoretical model in equation (10), although, as in the aggregated results, $a_2 = 2a_1$. This formulation in which Belgian-currency financing is a positive function of total-asset changes and a negative function of depreciation provisions accounts for about 70 per cent of the variation. The *t*-ratio for asset changes is significant at the 99 per cent level and for depreciation at the 93 per cent level. Using changes in current assets only in the second equation increases both the statistical significance of asset changes and the correlation ratio and the *a priori* restrictions are more readily satisfied. However, the *t*-ratio of the depreciation variable becomes insignificant. The third equation on net US-dollar financing of *BF* assets is particularly striking with all of the *t*-ratios of the variables of unitary significance and the coefficients have the correct signs. The coefficients satisfy the restriction that $a_1 = a_2 = a_3 = a_4 = 1$.

Table 7 Belgium–Luxembourg Economic Union

Dependent variable	Coefficient	Independent variable	t-ratio	R^2	Adjusted R^2	DW Statistic	Standard error estimate
(1) BL. F	23.37	Constant	0.58	0.70	0.62	2.11	60.0
	0.76	ΔA	4.06				
	-1.53	DEP	-2.13				
(2) BL. F	46.2	Constant	1.41	0.79	0.74	2.35	49.4
	1.0	ΔCA	5.30				
	-0.68	DEP	-1.47				
(3) BL. V'	-1.94	Constant	-0.82	0.99	0.99	2.50	3.2
	1.04	ΔA	51.34				
	-1.00	DEP	-17.68				
	-1.31	Π	-18.61				
	-0.91	F	-44.89				
(4) BL. V'	6.1	Constant	0.20	0.00	-0.24	2.06	67.2
	-2726.6	EX	-0.12				
	0.34	INT	0.02				
(5) BL. F	61.7	Constant	1.43	0.25	0.06	2.61	94.7
	21 231.5	EX	0.67				
	34.5	INT	1.59				
(6) BL. F	100.1	Constant	2.54	0.00	-0.11	2.47	102.8
	4.7	COINT	0.15				
(7) BL. V'	25.3	Constant	1.16	0.20	0.11	1.77	56.7
	-25.9	COINT	-1.51				

The simple, portfolio models, described on p. 105, were then applied to the BLEU data, yielding the results shown in Table 7, equations 4–7. For both foreign-currency funds and net US-dollar financing, actual exchange-rate changes and interest-rate differentials, even on a covered basis, were relatively insignificant as explanatory variables. Using the Chow test to examine the stability of the model between the two sub-periods, 1966–72 and 1973–6, it was found that the equation for net home-currency financing was stable (with a calculated $F = 23.8$ against a critical $F = 28.7$), but not the Belgian franc financing equation (where the calculated $F = 28.2$ and the critical $F = 11.4$).[10] This appears to be due to the much higher residual sum of squares in the second sub-period when, in 1974, Belgian financing declined slightly as total asset changes rose rapidly.

Canada

The Canadian results strongly support the theoretical model. Internal cash flow makes up the vast proportion of sources to finance asset changes (accounting for over 85 per cent of the total) with local Canadian funds providing the residual sources as in 1973 and 1974 (and averaging 17 per cent during the sample period). Net US parent-company contributions were negative except in 1966 (see Figs. 10–12), although gross US outflows were highly volatile compared to the reverse flow of repatriated dividends. Net US funds averaged −12 per cent of total-asset changes. The substantial increase in affiliate funds in 1976 may in part represent some US dollar financing (from financial holding subsidiaries) and so reflect an adaptation to 'exchange illusion' on the part of US investors in Canada.

The first regression in Table 8 yields highly significant results for the foreign-financing equation with the coefficients carrying the expected signs. The $R^2 = 0.91$. The asset change variable is of almost unitary significance whereas the depreciation term is significant at the 95 per cent level. Using current

---

[10] See the results of the Chow tests on the aggregated data.

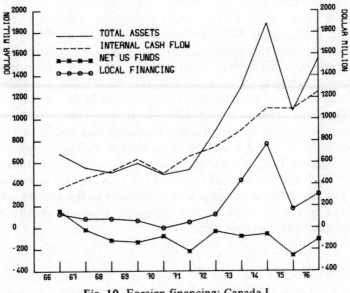

Fig. 10 Foreign financing: Canada I

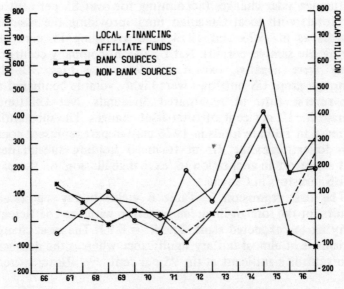

Fig. 11 Foreign financing: Canada II

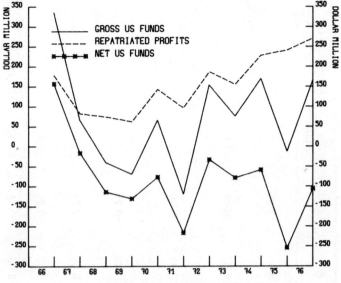

Fig. 12 Foreign financing: Canada III

assets only in the second equation, the statistical significance of the depreciation term declines into insignificance, even though the expected signs are retained. The poorer explanatory value of the depreciation variable may be explained by the importance of suppliers' credits as compared to other foreign financial sources (see Fig. 11). Therefore, the positive association with asset changes is not surprising nor the fact that increases in depreciation do not affect increases in Canadian funds from such sources. It explains 96 per cent of the variation in net US dollar financing of Canadian assets. The *a priori* restrictions, that $a_1 = a_2 = a_3 = a_4 = 1$, are also satisfied.

In the alternative, *post hoc* portfolio model, the coefficients of the exchange rates have the expected signs but not those of interest differentials in Table 8, equation 4. As shown in the fourth and fifth regressions, the results are not very significant, except for the interest rate differential in equation 4 with the wrong sign, and certainly much less so than the results of the model developed here. Likewise, the

Table 8. Canada

Dependent variable	Coefficient	Independent variable	t-ratio	R^2	Adjusted R^2	DW Statistic	Standard error estimate
(1) Can. F	-49.5	Constant	-0.60				
	0.57	ΔA	7.44				
	-0.76	DEP	-2.30	0.91	0.89	1.77	75.9
(2) Can. F	33.4	Constant	0.33				
	0.94	ΔCA	6.03				
	-0.43	DEP	-1.19	0.87	0.84	1.65	90.7
(3) Can. V'	50.0	Constant	2.44				
	0.81	ΔA	15.55				
	-1.20	DEP	-11.06				
	-0.75	Π	-6.65				
	-0.78	F	-12.08	0.99	0.99	2.11	12.2
(4) Can. V'	-85.0	Constant	2.18				
	747.9	EX	-0.43				
	-13.8	INT	-0.54	0.06	-0.18	1.20	116.9
(5) Can. F	199.1	Constant	2.37				
	476.3	EX	0.13				
	-2.41	INT	-0.04	0.00	-0.24	1.09	255.6
(6) Can. F	200.0	Constant	2.80				
	60.3	COINT	0.40	0.02	-0.09	1.17	236.4
(7) Can. V'	-82.6	Constant	-2.47				
	-50.9	COINT	-0.71	0.05	-0.05	1.31	110.4

portfolio model using covered interest differentials is statistically insignificant and both equations 6 and 7 have the wrong sign. As in the BLEU case, the Chow-test results indicate stability of the risk-reduction model between the two subperiods, 1966–72 and 1973–76, for net US financing (with a calculated $F = 9.8$ against a critical $F = 28.7$), but the stability hypothesis is rejected for Canadian financing in equation 1 by a small margin (where the calculated $F = 15.8$ and the critical $F = 11.4$). This appears to be due to the manner in which internal funds tended to reinforce the movement of Canadian-dollar financing in the latter sub-period, particularly in 1973–4, when inventories were being rapidly accumulated, financed by suppliers' credits, and profits also increased rapidly.

France

The French results strongly support the theoretical model. Local French borrowing is the residual used to finance assets when internal cash flow does not fully cover the financing needs and accounts, on average, for 34 per cent of asset changes. The net US contribution is slightly negative and declining (see Figs. 13 and 15) accounting for on average -11 per cent of asset changes. Repatriated dividends tend to increase steadily whereas gross US outflows are more erratic. Internal funds of US affiliates in France account for 73 per cent of asset changes from 1966 to 1976. It is particularly striking that in 1973 and 1974, when there were substantial increases in assets by US affiliates in France, these were financed largely by increases in French funds rather than US dollar outflows.

The first regression in Table 9 strongly confirms the basic model for foreign financing with the alternative, using current assets only in the second regression, being somewhat less significant. The *a priori*, second-order conditions that $a_1 = a_2 = 1$ are satisfied in the second equation. In the first, there is the familiar pattern of $a_2 = 2a_1$ where the coefficient of the depreciation term is about twice that of the asset change variable. As explained on p. 116, this is probably due

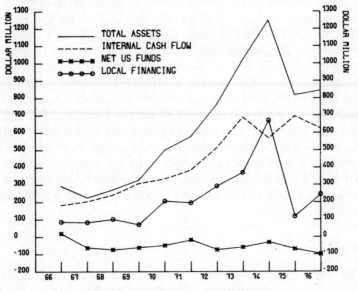

Fig. 13 Foreign financing: France I

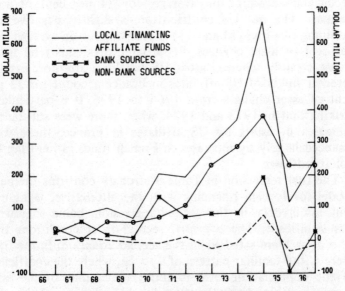

Fig. 14 Foreign financing: France II

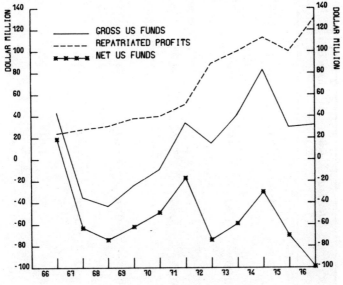

Fig. 15   Foreign financing: France III

to the fact that depreciation accounts for over half of internal funds and may statistically act as a proxy for cash flow. The third equation for net US-dollar financing is highly significant with the expected signs. All *t*-ratios are significant at the 99 per cent confidence level and the *a priori* restrictions are satisfied.

The *post hoc* portfolio model is quite insignificant in the fourth regression to explain US capital flows, with both the exchange-rate term and the interest-rate term carrying the wrong signs, although it is a great deal more significant in the fifth equation with the expected signs for the exchange-rate changes, and for the interest-rate differential, with the latter variable significant at the 95 per cent confidence level. Using the covered interest-rate differential in equation 6, the French franc financing variable carries the expected sign (i.e. US affiliates borrow francs as the covered differential favours franc borrowing relative to dollars) and is significant at the 87 per cent confidence level. There is strong evidence of serial auto-correlation in the two latter equations. In

Table 9 France

Dependent variable	Coefficient	Independent variable	t-ratio	R^2	Adjusted R^2	DW Statistic	Standard error estimate
(1) Fr. F	86.6	Constant	1.72	0.93	0.91	2.83	54.4
	0.87	ΔA	7.90				
	-1.74	DEP	-4.22				
(2) Fr. F	79.7	Constant	1.35	0.90	0.87	2.55	64.0
	0.87	ΔCA	6.55				
	-0.33	DEP	-1.03				
(3) Fr. V'	39.8	Constant	3.84	0.95	0.92	3.18	9.0
	9.92	ΔA	9.15				
	-1.34	DEP	-9.45				
	-0.82	Π	-7.98				
	-0.86	F	-8.20				
(4) Fr. V'	-39.9	Constant	-2.10	0.07	-0.16	1.67	34.9
	-260.7	EX	-0.42				
	-7.0	INT	-0.80				
(5) Fr. F	49.0	Constant	0.65	0.52	0.40	1.18	137.0
	441.0	EX	0.18				
	90.7	INT	2.79				
(6) Fr. F	258.0	Constant	5.06	0.29	0.22	1.04	157.2
	-52.5	COINT	-1.94				
(7) Fr. V'	-54.8	Constant	5.03	0.03	-0.07	1.52	33.6
	3.24	COINT	0.56				

Table 9, equation 7, the net home-currency variable carries the expected sign but is insignificant. As in the BLEU and Canadian cases above, the Chow-test results indicate the stability of equation 3 over the two sub-periods, 1966–72 and 1973–6 (with a calculated $F = 6.1$ against a critical $F = 28.7$), but not for equation 1, French financing (where the calculated $F = 39.2$ and the critical $F = 11.4$). However, in the latter case, this appears to be due to the very low residual sum of squares in the 1973–6 sub-period, whereas the model is less significant for the foreign-financing equation in the earlier sub-period where internal funds and French financing move in a similar fashion.

Germany

In Figs. 16–18, the data on financing of US direct investment in Germany conform more or less to the pattern observed in other countries with internal cash flow (85.6 per cent of asset changes) as supplemented by borrowing in Germany (29 per cent) financing almost all of the asset changes. The net contribution in US dollars was negative for all years except 1966, averaging about −18 per cent over the sample period. 1971 was the only year in which gross US outflows seemed to deviate substantially from a basically declining pattern (see Fig. 18).

The statistical results for Germany (Table 10), at first appear to be rather curious. The first equation is not highly significant although the coefficients carry the expected signs. The explanation for this may be, in part, found in the results of the second regression where 91 per cent of the variation in Deutsche Mark financing can be explained by inventory changes and changes in depreciation provisions. It could be that in Germany total-asset changes themselves are in part determined by financial or, at least, exchange-rate considerations so that local liabilities are not so much associated with total-asset changes as with inventory changes only, which alone would account for 90 per cent of the variation in German currency financing (especially since suppliers' credits are the dominant source of local borrowing in Germany).

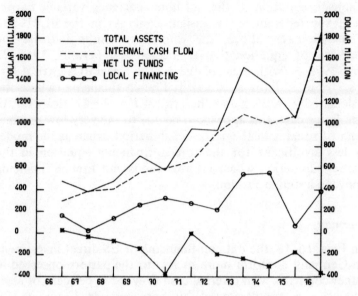

Fig. 16 Foreign financing: Germany I

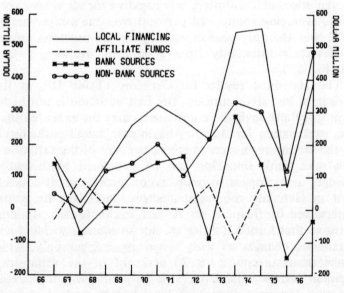

Fig. 17 Foreign financing: Germany II

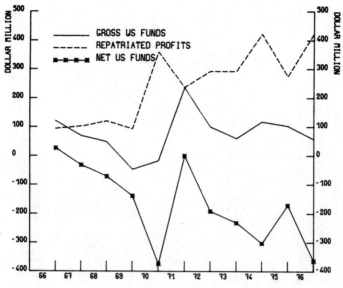

Fig. 18 Foreign financing: Germany III

In the second equation, the depreciation term carries the wrong sign, but is not significant. On the other hand, the third regression for net US-dollar financing has the expected signs, satisfies the *a priori* restrictions and is highly significant with all of the *t*-ratios of the explanatory variables being significant above the 99 per cent confidence level.

Particularly interesting in the case of Germany, are the results of the alternative, portfolio models. What is important and not contrary to the learning process postulated earlier is the quite different behaviour revealed by dividing 1966–76 into two periods. In the fourth regression, from 1966–76, the *post hoc* portfolio model is totally insignificant in explaining net US outflows, but it becomes a significant explanation for 94 per cent of the variation in net US capital outflows from 1973 to 1976 in Table 10, equation 5. Even so, the risk-reduction model in equation 3 still yields more significant results. The portfolio model is fairly weak in explaining German financing (in the sixth regression) although a similar time division could be made. One implication of

Table 10 Germany

Dependent variable	Coefficient	Independent variable	t-ratio	R^2	Adjusted R^2	DW Statistic	Standard error estimate
(1) Gr. F	108.9	Constant	1.03	0.61	0.51	1.57	123.4
	0.44	ΔA	2.92				
	−0.65	DEP	−1.42				
(2) Gr. F	77.1	Constant	1.52	0.91	0.88	1.44	60.0
	0.94	Δ Inventory	7.88				
	0.21	DEP	1.67				
(3) Gr. V'	50.2	Constant	1.98	0.98	0.96	2.73	27.9
	0.95	ΔA	10.08				
	−1.17	DEP	−8.86				
	−0.87	Π	10.81				
	−1.11	F	−11.15				
(4) Gr. V'	−110.8	Constant	1.23	0.08	−0.15	1.87	151.2
	−1928.5	EX	−0.77				
(5) Gr. V' (1973–6)	−731.9	Constant	−5.85	0.94	0.84	2.32	33.7
	4588.5	EX	4.19				
	−210.8	INT	−3.51				
(6) Gr. F	202.2	Constant	1.98	0.23	0.04	2.46	172.5
	4348.9	EX	1.53				
(7) Gr. F	256.3	Constant	4.08	0.02	−0.09	1.70	183.9
	22.1	COINT	0.42				
(8) Gr. V'	−180.5	Constant	−3.60	0.02	−0.08	1.37	146.9
	19.9	COINT	0.47				

these results is that a portfolio adjustment model may only apply to non-financial investors in times of extreme exchange rate turmoil where the possible exchange losses become so apparent and significant that 'exchange illusion' is dropped as the cost of its continued acceptance increases. It could be mentioned that nominal interest-rate differentials generally favoured German borrowing as against US capital flows (as in Table 10, regressions 4–5), but, given the inflation rate differentials, a positive sign indicates money illusion on the part of US investors. The positive sign on the EX coefficient in Table 10, equation 5 indicates that as the Deutsche Mark strengthened from 1973–6, US investors were highly reluctant to maintain (much less increase) dollar liabilities to finance DM assets – behaviour which is not profitable and can only be explained by 'exchange illusion'. Similarly, while the covered differential models are insignificant, the coefficient in Table 10, equation 7 carries the wrong sign. The Chow-test results confirm the stability of the risk-reduction model applied to Table 10, equation 1 on the foreign financing of US direct investment in Germany (with a calculated $F = 3.4$ and a critical $F = 11.4$), but not for equation 3 on net US financing (where the calculated $F = 133.7$ against a critical $F = 28.7$). The possible instability of the parameters of the model over time in the latter case probably reflect the learning process in which firms, while still having exchange illusion in their home currency, individually assess the costs of using different currencies to finance foreign assets (as discussed on p. 67). In the German case, it was not dollar liabilities that increased in the latter period, but, rather, that internal funds were increasingly relied upon as opposed to funds borrowed in Deutsche Mark.

Italy

The pattern of financing of US direct investment in Italy is much the same as in the other countries except that due to a low level of internal cash flow to finance asset changes, especially from 1970 until 1975, local Italian sources of financing are almost as important as internal funds, except in

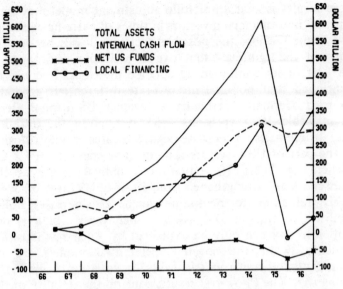

Fig. 19 Foreign financing: Italy I

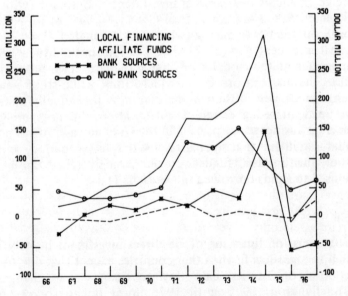

Fig. 20 Foreign financing: Italy II

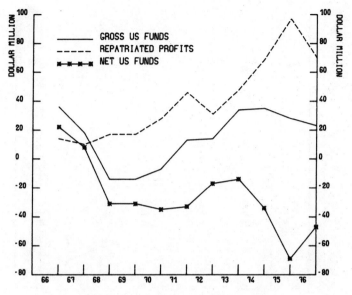

Fig. 21 Foreign financing: Italy III

1975 and 1976 (see Figs. 19–21). Internal funds accounted for 69.5 per cent of asset changes over the period 1966–76, but 55 per cent from 1970–4, whereas Italian financial sources accounted for 34 per cent of the total over the sample period, but for 47 per cent from 1970–4. Thus, foreign funds were the main residual when internal sources were inadequate to finance asset changes. Net US dollar financing was negative except in 1966–7 when Italian sources were negative due to net repayments on bank loans.

Along with the Canadian, French and Dutch results for foreign financing, the Italian results in the first regression in Table 11 are the most supportive of the theoretical model. The *a priori* restrictions are satisfied. The alternative using current assets only is considerably less significant, especially the depreciation term. The third regression for US financing is highly significant with the expected signs. The *a priori* restrictions on the coefficients are also satisfied.

The results of the *post hoc* portfolio model in Table 11, regressions 4 and 5 are not very significant, despite the

Table 11 Italy

Dependent variable	Coefficient	Independent variable	t-ratio	R^2	Adjusted R^2	DW Statistic	Standard error estimate
(1) It. F	-2.88	Constant	-0.18	0.95	0.94	2.24	23.6
	0.80	ΔA	12.17				
	-1.07	DEP	-6.09				
(2) It. F	21.8	Constant	0.80	0.85	0.82	1.80	41.8
	0.86	ΔCA	6.46				
	-0.19	DEP	-0.79				
(3) It. V'	1.94	Constant	0.28	0.91	0.84	2.39	9.97
	1.16	ΔA	6.18				
	-1.41	DEP	-5.80				
	-1.26	Π	-6.34				
	-0.99	F	-5.68				
(4) It. V'	-18.3	Constant	-1.76	0.16	-0.04	1.27	25.5
	117 114.9	EX	1.24				
	1.7	INT	0.71				
(5) It. F	59.4	Constant	1.58	0.29	0.11	1.22	92.1
	-486 986.7	EX	-1.42				
	-15.4	INT	-1.79				

weakening of the lira in dollar terms during most of the observation period (see Table 5, p. 123) and the wide, nominal interest-rate differentials. Both considerations would have led to predictions of positive correlations with US outflows during most of the observation period. The portfolio model does carry the expected signs and the *t*-ratios in equation 5 would indicate that the variables may have some limited significance in explaining the financing of direct investment. There is evidence of serial auto-correlation in the portfolio-adjustment equations. Due to a lack of available data, it was not possible to test an alternative model using covered interest rate differentials. The Chow-test results would indicate that the model is stable between the two sub-periods, 1966–72 and 1973–6 (with the foreign-financing equation having a calculated $F = 0.8$ against a critical $F = 11.4$, and the net home-currency financing equation showing a calculated $F = 4.8$ against a critical $F = 18.7$). For the foreign-financing model, the Italian equation is the most stable of the seven currency areas.

Netherlands

The data for the Netherlands display a similar pattern to the other countries with internal cash-flow financing almost the totality of asset changes, especially since 1972, with local Dutch borrowing as a residual (see Fig. 22). Foreign borrowing was composed almost entirely of supplier credits, especially after 1972. The net US dollar contribution declined steadily over the observation period and was negative after 1970. On average, over the sample period 1966–76, internal funds accounted for 79.8 per cent of asset changes, Dutch funds accounting for 24 per cent and net US funds for 5.4 per cent.

In Table 12, the first equation for the Netherlands reflects the basic theoretical model for foreign financing and is highly significant at the 99 per cent confidence level with the expected signs. The *a priori* restrictions are satisfied. The alternative in the second equation using current assets only is considerably less significant, especially for the depreciation

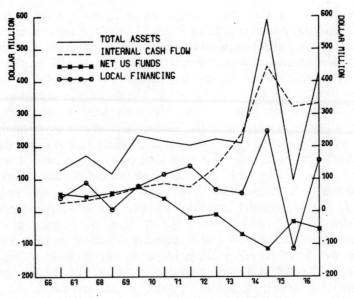

Fig. 22 Foreign financing: Netherlands I

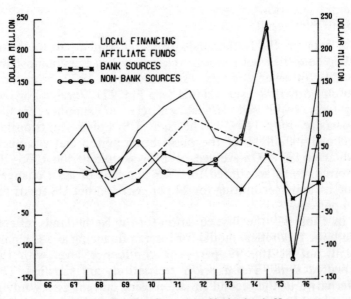

Fig. 23 Foreign financing: Netherlands II

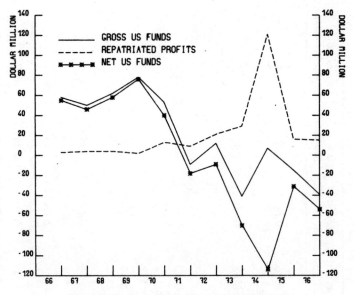

Fig. 24 Foreign financing: Netherlands III

term. The third regression for US-dollar financing displays significant results with the correct signs. The *a priori* restrictions are readily satisfied using the Wald test. The Durbin–Watson statistics in the first and third equations are in the indeterminant range so that the possible presence of autocorrelated error terms cannot be dismissed.

The fourth equation in Table 11 employing the alternative *post hoc* portfolio model is revealing as the strengthening guilder exerted a negative influence on US-capital outflows to finance appreciating – in dollar terms – Dutch assets. As with Germany, the results are particularly significant after 1972, but once again, the results indicate a degree of 'exchange illusion' in which all exchange-rate changes – even profitable ones in home-currency terms – are considered as increasing the risk of home-currency profits. The fifth regression using the *post hoc* portfolio model on Dutch funds is insignificant, as are the sixth and seventh equations using the covered interest differentials (although the latter carries the expected signs). The Chow test for stability

Table 12 Netherlands

Dependent variable	Coefficient	Independent variable	t-ratio	R^2	Adjusted R^2	DW Statistic	Standard error estimate
(1) Nth. F	-15.5	Constant	-0.63	0.86	0.82	1.38	38.4
	0.80	ΔA	6.52				
	-1.18	DEP	-3.07				
(2) Nth. F	52.5	Constant	1.44	0.68	0.60	1.91	57.8
	0.66	ΔCA	3.78				
	-0.34	DEP	-0.72				
(3) Nth. V'	28.7	Constant	1.25	0.93	0.89	1.28	20.4
	0.73	ΔA	3.13				
	-0.86	DEP	-2.45				
	-0.71	Π	-3.28				
	-0.92	F	-3.31				
(4) Nth. V'	1.8	Constant	0.08	0.34	0.18	1.12	55.9
	-3935.3	EX	-1.82				
	-41.2	INT	-1.19				
(5) Nth. F	105.6	Constant	2.83	0.12	-0.09	2.77	95.9
	1524.6	EX	0.41				
	48.9	INT	0.82				
(6) Nth. F	75.8	Constant	2.58	0.05	-0.06	3.22	94.4
	-3.58	COINT	-0.65				
(7) Nth. V'	-0.37	Constant	-0.02	0.01	-0.10	0.44	64.7
	1.12	COINT	0.30				

indicates that the model developed in this study is stable as applied to the Netherlands, over the two sub-periods, 1966–72 and 1973–6 (with the foreign-financing equation showing a calculated $F = 5.2$ against a critical $F = 11.4$, and the net home-currency financing equation having a calculated $F = 1.1$ against a critical $F = 18.7$). For the net US-financing equation, it is the most stable of the seven currency areas.

United Kingdom

The pattern of financing of US-owned affiliates in the UK diverges to some extent from that of the other countries, perhaps due in part to the longer period of operations in the UK in which relatively few companies in the sample were new to the UK economy in the 1960s. The erratic changes in total assets over the sample period were financed principally by internal funds but in a fluctuating manner, whereas UK-borrowing acted as the residual source of financing (see Figs. 25–27). Because of the long-standing nature of most US investments in the UK economy, net US capital flows were negative but irregular over the entire period. On average over the sample period, internal funds accounted for 96 per cent of total sources financing asset changes, whereas net US funds accounted for −18 per cent and UK funds for 16 per cent (although the latter were highly negative in two years, 1972 and 1975). Large net repayments to UK banks took place in 1972 and 1975 and may have been related, in part, to the introduction of the supplementary reserve requirements (i.e. the corset) on bank lending in 1973 which would have had a restrictive impact on local borrowing. In those two years, internal funds were in substantial excess of total-asset changes. Due perhaps in part to exchange-rate pressures on sterling in 1972 and 1975, gross US outflows were insignificant, so that with normal levels of dividend payments, net US dollar contributions reached their most negative amounts since the 1967 devaluation of the pound (see Fig. 27). Funds from other affiliates also dropped in 1972, but increased substantially in 1975 and were probably chosen in preference to dollar financing, in the absence of the

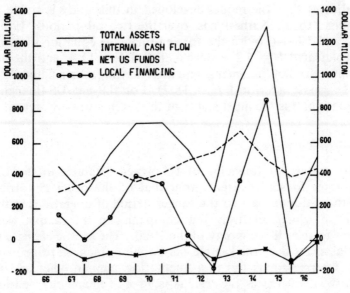

Fig. 25 Foreign financing: UK I

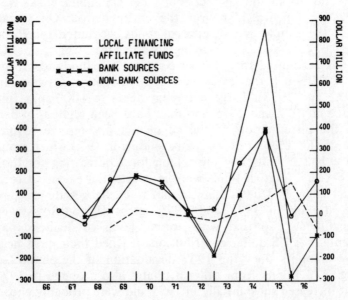

Fig. 26 Foreign financing: UK II

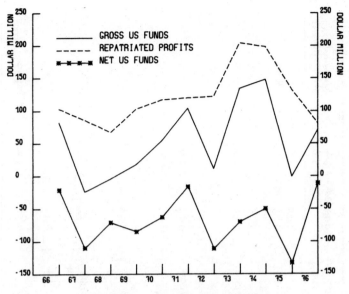

Fig. 27 Foreign financing: UK III

availability of sterling financing, in accordance with the risk-reduction hypothesis.

The first regression on the foreign financing of UK assets in Table 13 conforms to the theoretical model with the asset-change variable significant at the 99 per cent confidence level and the depreciation term, carrying the expected sign, significant at the 94 per cent level. The alternative formulation in Table 13, equation 2, using current assets only is slightly less significant for asset changes and the depreciation term is considerably less significant, while still carrying the expected signs. The lower significance of the depreciation terms may be related to the limitations on the use of sterling funds so that US affiliates in the UK may have increased borrowings, even when internal funds increased, in anticipation of possible restrictions. Bank financing is also quite important for US affiliates in the UK (see Fig. 26), so that the availability of extensive overdraft facilities may favour the use of external funds relative to countries where more traditional bank loans have to be negotiated.

Table 13 United Kingdom

Dependent variable	Coefficient	Independent variable	t-ratio	R^2	Adjusted R^2	DW Statistic	Standard error estimate
(1) UK. F	-118.7	Constant	-1.08	0.93	0.91	1.65	87.0
	0.91	ΔA	10.33				
	-0.94	DEP	-2.17				
(2) UK. F	21.4	Constant	0.16	0.89	0.86	1.80	109.5
	0.95	ΔCA	8.02				
	-1.19	DEP	-0.34				
(3) UK. V'	-33.5	Constant	-1.64	0.93	0.89	1.98	13.5
	0.82	ΔA	8.88				
	-0.94	DEP	-7.74				
	-0.73	Π	-7.48				
	-0.78	F	-8.37				
(4) UK. V'	-71.9	Constant	-2.92	0.03	-0.21	2.61	45.0
	-42.4	EX	-0.32				
	0.30	INT	0.02				
(5) UK. F	218.4	Constant	1.21	0.01	-0.23	2.06	328.5
	142.8	EX	0.15				
	-8.5	INT	-0.10				
(6) UK. F	102.0	Constant	1.01	0.20	0.11	1.92	279.2
	-122.7	COINT	-1.49				
(7) UK. V'	-69.0	Constant	-4.44	0.00	-0.11	2.64	42.9
	-2.5	COINT	-0.20				

The third equation in Table 13 for net US dollar financing is statistically significant with 93 per cent of the variation explained by the model. The *t*-ratios are all significant at the 99 per cent confidence level and the coefficients have the expected signs. Using the Wald test, the *a priori* restrictions are easily satisfied. The relatively low value of the coefficient of the profit variable may be explained by the sudden decline in profitability of UK affiliates starting in 1974 (both relative to the past — on average 4.5 per cent return on sales from 1966 to 1973 to 1.2 per cent from 1974 to 1976 — and relative to other countries), implied that fewer profits were available relative to investment needs and were offset with sterling borrowing where this was administratively feasible.

The UK results support strongly the risk-reduction hypothesis. The alternative, *post hoc* portfolio model in Table 13, equations 4 and 5 are statistically insignificant in explaining the financing of US direct investment in the UK. Equation 6 using the alternative portfolio model with covered interest differentials to explain sterling financing does carry the expected sign, but is of limited significance, whereas the results of equation 7 are of no significance. The Chow-test results show that the risk-reduction model is stable between the two sub-periods, 1966–72 and 1973–76 (with the foreign-financing equation showing a calculated $F = 4.3$ against a critical $F = 11.4$, and the net home-currency financing equation showing a calculated $F = 1.3$ against a critical $F = 28.7$).

VIII CONCLUSION

The purpose of this study has been to explain the determinants of capital flows financing foreign direct investment. More specifically, it has assessed the various means by which multinational enterprises finance their additional foreign asset acquisitions by examining respectively the determinants of net home-currency funds, foreign-currency borrowings and foreign-generated internal cash flows of foreign affiliates. The main hypothesis – developed and tested above – suggests that, with regard to the currency denomination of capital flows financing direct investment, it is not the expectations of exchange-rate changes in themselves that primarily determine the direction and magnitude of capital flows, but rather, for direct investors, the fact that all foreign currency denominated assets involve a perceived risk for firms maximizing their consolidated profits in terms of home-country currency. This risk perception leads direct investors to have 'exchange-rate illusion' in their choice of liabilities to finance foreign assets, implying a higher degree of segmentation in international capital markets than is normally assumed in portfolio-adjustment theories applied to capital movements. The costs of overcoming these market imperfections act as a constraint on the otherwise portfolio-optimizing behaviour of rational, non-financial companies.

This study of the determinants of foreign-asset financing by direct investors produces results which have some important implications for both capital movement theory and for our understanding of the financial behaviour of multinational enterprises.

Contrary to the expectations of those theorists who view exchange risks attached to assets in individual currencies, the present study would contend that instead a foreign non-financial investor distinguishes more crudely between home-country and foreign currencies in general. Obviously, this will not apply to all non-financial investors whose levels of sophistication will certainly vary nor is it likely to apply over time as investors learn to be more discriminating in their choice of currency financing. 'Exchange illusion' may even eventually be lost concerning the use of the home-country currency. The depreciation of the US dollar against certain 'strong' currencies (Deutsche Mark, Swiss franc, yen, guilder, etc.) especially since 1977, may have precipitated the loss of exchange illusion for many American direct investors and even more so for their bankers and accountants. In fact, the empirical results of this study, which strongly support the risk-reduction hypothesis stemming from exchange illusion, may reflect a recognition lag on the part of the US direct investors that the dollar has fallen from its pinnacle as the perennially 'strong' currency.

Empirically, the surprise result is that over most of the sample period, 1966–76, the group of American companies (including many of the biggest names in manufacturing) on the whole treated so-called weak currencies and strong currencies in a similar manner. Except towards the end of the observation period when investors might have become somewhat more sophisticated, the decisions to finance asset changes with home or foreign currencies were made according to the same criteria and in the same proportions in Germany and the Netherlands as in Italy or the UK. In all cases, risk reduction in terms of exchange rate exposure, rather than portfolio-adjustment criteria, best explained the currency denomination of capital flows financing direct investment.

Theoretically, the model developed here leads to a new assessment of the assumptions of many capital-movement theories which rely upon a high degree of capital-market integration or perfect information. The present theory, as supported by the empirical results, would suggest that market segmentation is or at least has been much greater than is normally assumed. The level of investor sophistication has been such that for most non-financial companies, the world still is divided into home and abroad with this distinction carrying over into notions towards risk. Assets denominated in foreign currencies are viewed as riskier to companies reporting profits in home currency than similar domestic assets. The world of perfect capital mobility with capital as an international phenomenon cannot be seen in this study. Despite protracted discussion of multinational enterprise and the growth of international investment, it is contended that capital is still very much a national phenomenon. There is little evidence in this study that multinational firms use their potential financial power to manoeuver funds between currencies in pursuit of speculative gain (or to avoid losses) except in unusually unstable circumstances. The theoretical model developed here, however, does allow for three increasing levels of financial sophistication ranging from firms who view all foreign currencies at risk (the principal behaviour observed in this study) to those who distinguish risks between various foreign currencies but not that of the home currency (a behaviour for which there is some evidence towards the end of the observation period) to, finally, super-sophisticated firms who even view the home currency at risk and who therefore have no exchange illusion (a behaviour not observed in this study for non-financial companies).

The conclusions of this study should be viewed as tentative. While a plausible theory of foreign-asset financing is developed for direct investors, the decisions affecting balance-sheet relationships are highly complex. A simple model specifying a few causal relationships can only shed light on part of this process. In particular, the theoretical model is based on certain key assumptions including: the profit-maximizing behaviour of firms, the exogeneity of the asset investment decisions with internal cash flow of affiliates as given, that hedging for currency exposure takes place through balance-sheet adjustments rather than in the forward market, and the covariance of changes in bilateral, nominal exchange rates is zero. Useful, future research might be directed towards the elaboration of more sophisticated models which relax some of these simplifying assumptions, particularly the one in which the exchange rate is a random variable.

The simple theoretical model of risk reduction is strongly supported by the empirical results, but it should be noted that the empirical tests are limited in time, scope and geographical coverage. Direct investors of other home countries, of other industries (such as petroleum), operating in other regions (outside of the OECD area), or at other times, might behave differently. With these qualifications, however, the results of the present study would indicate that multinational enterprises attempt to avoid perceived exchange risks in the financing of their foreign operations. As a result, they will use foreign-currency borrowing as the residual source of financing, after the foreign-generated cash flow of affiliates, as a positive function of asset changes and a negative function of depreciation allowances (normally the source of internal funds). Net home-currency financing of foreign assets is usually small or negative, only becoming significant as a source of funds when asset growth is very rapid, past investments are small, profits are small or negative, or when foreign borrowing is limited or unavailable.

This study has not addressed itself directly to the balance-of-payments' impact of the financial behaviour of multinational enterprises. To do so would require a much more comprehensive theoretical approach than the one developed above which would have to include all of those interdependent financial flows of these firms, including trade transactions, liquid-asset management, royalty and interest flows, etc. In particular, the present theory does not necessarily imply that MNEs would remain indifferent to the currency risk exposure of their liquid assets in the very short run. With this limitation in mind, however, the theory developed here can, by extension, contribute to our understanding of the narrower, but important, question of the impact on the balance of payments of flows financing foreign direct investments. These flows would seem to be generally positive for home countries and negative for host countries, with the actual capital flows involved being very low relative to the size of the asset changes.

BIBLIOGRAPHY

Adler, M., 'The Cost of Capital and Valuation of a Two-country Firm', *Journal of Finance*, March 1974.

Agmon, T. and Lessard, D., 'Investor Recognition of Corporate International Diversification', *Journal of Finance*, Sept. 1977.

Aliber, R. Z., 'A Theory of Direct Foreign Investment', in Kindleberger, C. P. (ed.), *The International Corporation: A Symposium*, Cambridge, Mass.: MIT Press, 1970.

Arndt, S. W., 'International Short-Term Capital Movements: A Distributed Lag Model of Speculation in Foreign Exchange', *Econometrica*, January 1968, pp. 59–70.

Baret, J., 'Record of Discussion', in Borch, K. and Mossin, J. (eds.), *Risk and Uncertainty*, New York: Macmillan, 1968.

Barlow, E. R. and Wender, I. T., *Foreign Investment and Taxation*, Englewood Cliffs, N.J.: Prentice-Hall, Inc., 1955.

Baumol, W. J., 'Speculation, Profitability and Stability', *Review of Economics and Statistics*, August 1957, pp. 263–71.

Bell, P. W., 'Private Capital Movements and the United States Balance of Payments', *Factors Affecting the United States Balance of Payments*, Joint Economic Committee, 87th Congress, 1962.

Berlin, P. D., *Foreign Affiliate Financial Survey, 1966–1969*, Office of Foreign Direct Investments, United States Department of Commerce, July 1971.

Borts, G. H., 'Long-Run Capital Movements', in Dunning, J. H. (ed.), *Economic Analysis and the Multinational Enterprise*, London: George Allen and Unwin, 1974.

Branson, W. H., *Financial Capital Flows in the United States Balance of Payments*, Amsterdam: North Holland, 1968.

Brooke, M. Z. and Remmers, H. L., *The Strategy of Multinational Enterprise*, London: Longman, 1971.

Buckley, P. and Casson, M., *The Future of the Multinational Enterprise*, London: Macmillan, 1976.

Bursk, E. C., Dearden, J., Hawkins, D. F., and Longstreet, U. M., *Financial Control of Multinational Operations*, New York: Financial Executives Research Foundation, 1971.

Caves, R. E., 'International Corporations: The Industrial Economics of Foreign Investment', *Economica*, February 1971, pp. 1–27; reprinted in Dunning, J. H. (ed.), *International Investment*, Harmondsworth: Penguin Books, 1972.

Cohen, B. J., 'A Survey of Capital Movements and Findings Regarding their Interest Sensitivity', *Factors Affecting the United States Balance of Payments*, Hearings before the Joint Economic Committee, 87th Congress, July 1963.

Dunning, J. H., 'The Determinants of International Production', *Oxford Economic Papers*, November 1973, pp. 289–336.

Dunning, J. H., 'Multinational Enterprises and Domestic Capital Formation', in Wilson, J. S. G. and Scheffer, C. F. (eds.), *Multinational Enterprises – Financial and Monetary Aspects*, Leiden: A. W. Sijthoff, 1974.

Feder, G. and Regev, U., 'International Loans, Direct Foreign Investment, and Optimal Capital Accumulation', *The Economic Record*, September 1975.

Feldstein, M. S., 'Mean-variance Analysis in the Theory of Liquidity Preference and Portfolio Selection', *Review of Economic Studies*, January 1969.

Floyd, J. E., 'International Capital Movements and Monetary Equilibrium', *American Economic Review*, September 1969.

Goldsbrough, D. J., 'The Role of Foreign Direct Investment in the External Adjustment Process', *IMF Staff Papers*, December 1979.

Hartman, D. G., 'Foreign Investment and Finance with Risk', *Quarterly Journal of Economics*, May 1979.

Heckerman, D. G., 'Exchange Rate Systems and the Efficient Allocation of Risk', *Proceedings of a Symposium on Trade, Growth and Balance of Payments*, University of Chicago, December 1970.

Hendershott, P. H., 'International Short-term Capital Movements: Comment IV', *American Economic Review*, June 1967.

Hood, N. and Young, S., *The Economics of the Multinational Enterprise*, London: Longman, 1979.

Hume, D., *Essays and Treatises on Several Subjects*, vol. I, 1752.

Hymer, S. H., *The International Operations of National Firms: A Study of Direct Foreign Investments*, Ph.D., MIT, 1960: subsequently published by MIT Press, 1976.

International Monetary Fund, *Balance of Payments Manual*, 4th edition, Washington: IMF, 1977.

Johnson, H. G., 'The Transfer Problems and Exchange Stability', *Journal of Political Economy*, June 1956.

Johnson, H. G., 'Some Aspects of the Theory of Economic Policy in a World of Capital Mobility', in Bagiotti, T. (ed.), *Essays in Honour of Marco Fanno*, Padua: Cedam, 1966.

Johnston, J., *Econometric Methods*, 1st edition, New York: McGraw-Hill, 1963.

Kenen, P. B., 'Short-term Capital Movements and the United States Balance of Payments', *Factors Affecting the United States Balance of Payments*, Hearings before the Joint Economic Committee, 87th Congress, July 1963.

Kenen, P. B., 'Capital Mobility and Financial Integration: A Survey',

Princeton Studies in International Finance, no. 39, Princeton University, 1976.

Kindleberger, C. P., *Europe and the Dollar*, Cambridge, Mass.: MIT Press, 1966.

Kindleberger, C. P., *American Business Abroad*, New Haven, Conn.: Yale University Press, 1969.

Kindleberger, C. P., 'Money Illusion and Foreign Exchange', in Bergsten, C. F. and Tyler, W. G., *Leading Issues in International Policy*, Lexington, Mass.: D. C. Heath, 1975.

Kouri, P. J. K. and Porter, M. G., 'International Capital Flows and Portfolio Equilibrium', *Journal of Political Economy*, June 1974.

Ladenson, M., 'A Dynamic Balance Sheet Approach to American Direct Foreign Investment', *International Economic Review*, October 1972.

Laffargue, J.-P., 'Une explication économique des flux d'investissements directs entre pays hautement industrialisés', *Revue économique*, May 1971.

Leamer, E. E. and Stern, R. M., *Quantitative International Economics*, Boston: Allyn, and Bacon, 1970.

Leamer, E. E. and Stern, R. M., 'Problems in the Theory and Empirical Estimation of International Capital Movements', in Machlup, F., Salant, W. S., and Tarshis, L. (eds.), *International Mobility and Movement of Capital*, NBER, New York: Columbia University Press, 1972.

Lorenson, L., *Reporting Foreign Operations in Dollars*, New York: American Institute of Certified Public Accountants, 1972.

Lunn, J., 'Determinants of United States Direct Investment in the E.E.C.: Further Evidence', *European Economic Review*, January 1980.

Manser, W. A. P., *The Financial Role of Multinational Enterprise*, London: Cassell, 1973.

Mantel, I. M., 'Sources and Uses of Funds of Majority-Owned Foreign Affiliates of U.S. Companies, 1973–1976', *Bureau of Economic Analyses Staff Paper*, May 1979.

Markowitz, H. M., 'Portfolio Selection', *Journal of Finance*, March 1952.

Meade, J. E., *The Balance of Payments, The Theory of International Economic Policy*, vol. I, London: Oxford University Press, 1951.

Modigliani, F. and Miller, M. H., 'The Cost of Capital, Corporation Finance and the Theory of Investment', *American Economic Review*, June 1958.

Modigliani, F. and Miller, M. H., 'Corporate Income Taxes and the Cost of Capital: A Correction', *American Economic Review*, June 1963.

Mundell, R. A., 'The Monetary Dynamics of International Adjustment under Fixed and Flexible Exchange Rates', *Quarterly Journal of Economics*, May 1960.

Neufeld, E. P., *A Global Corporation: A History of the International Development of Massey-Ferguson Limited*, Toronto: University of

Toronto Press, 1969.

Organisation for Economic Co-operation and Development, *Economic Outlook*, OECD, no. 24, December 1978.

Organisation for Economic Co-operation and Development, *International Direct Investment: Policies, Procedures and Practices*, Paris: OECD, 1979.

Organisation for Economic Co-operation and Development, *Declaration on International Investment and Multinational Enterprises*, Paris: OECD, June 1976.

Organisation for Economic Co-operation and Development, *Main Economic Indicators*, Paris: OECD, Historical Series, various issues.

Penrose, E. T., 'Foreign Investment and the Growth of the Firm', *Economic Journal*, June 1956.

Plasschaert, S., 'Multinational Companies and International Capital Markets', in Wilson, J. S. G. and Scheffer, C. F. (eds.), *Multinational Enterprises - Financial and Monetary Aspects*, Leiden: A. W. Sijthoff, 1974.

Polak, J. J., 'Monetary Analysis of Income Formation and Payments Problems', *IMF Staff Papers*, November 1957.

Polk, J., Meister, I. W., and Veit, L. A., *United States Production Abroad and the Balance of Payments*, New York: The Conference Board, 1968.

Porter, M. G., 'Capital Flows as an Offset to Monetary Policy: The German Case', *IMF Staff Papers*, July 1972.

Rhomberg, R. R., 'Canada's Foreign Exchange Market: A Quarterly Model', *IMF Staff Papers*, April 1960.

Rhomberg, R. P., 'A Model of the Canadian Economy under Fixed and Fluctuating Exchange Rates', *Journal of Political Economy*, February, 1964.

Ricardo, D., *On the Principles of Political Economy and Taxation*, 1817.

Ricks, D. A., *International Dimensions of Corporate Finance*, Englewood Cliffs, N.J.: Prentice-Hall, 1978.

Robbins, S. M. and Stobaugh, R. B., 'Comments', in Machlup, F., Salant, W. S., and Tarshis, L. (eds.), *International Mobility and Movement of Capital*, NBER, New York: Columbia University Press, 1972, pages 354–65.

Robbins, S. M. and Stobaugh, R. B., *Money in the Multinational Enterprise*, New York: Basic Books, 1973.

Robinson, J., *Economic Heresies*, London: Macmillan, 1971.

Robock, S. H., Simmonds, K., and Zwick, J., *International Business and Multinational Enterprises*, Homewood, Illinois: Richard D. Irwin, Inc., 1977 revised edition.

Rugman, A. M., 'Internationalisation as a General Theory of Foreign Direct Investment: A Re-appraisal of the Literature', *Weltwirtschaftliches Archiv*, vol. 116, no. 2, 1980.

Shapiro, A., 'Financial Structure and Cost of Capital in the Multinational

Corporation', *Journal of Financial and Quantitative Analysis*, June 1978.

Stein, J. L., 'International Short-term Capital Movements', *American Economic Review*, March 1965.

Stevens, G. V. G., 'Capital Mobility and the International Firm', in Machlup, F., Salant, W. S. and Tarshis, L. (eds.), *International Mobility and Movement of Capital*, NEBR, New York: Columbia University Press, 1972.

Stevens, G. V. G., 'The Determinants of Investment', in Dunning, J. H., (ed.), *Economic Analysis and the Multinational Enterprise*, London: George Allen and Unwin, 1974.

Stiglitz, J., 'A Re-examination of the Modigliani–Miller Theorem', *American Economic Review*, December 1969.

Taussig, F. W., *International Trade*, New York: Macmillan, 1927.

Tobin, J. E., 'Liquidity Preference as Behaviour Towards Risk', *Review of Economic Studies*, February 1958.

Tsiang, S. C., 'The Theory of Foreward Exchange and Effects of Government Intervention on the Forward Exchange Market', *IMF Staff Papers*, April 1959.

United States Senate, *Multinational Corporations in the Dollar Devaluation Crisis*, Staff Report for the Subcommittee on Multinational Corporations, United States Senate, 94th Session, June 1975.

United States Tariff Commission for the Committee on Finance, United States Senate, *Implications of Multinational Firms for World Trade and Investment and for United States Trade and Labour*, 93rd Congress, 1st Session, Washington: February 1973.

Vernon, R., 'International Investment and International Trade in the Product Cycle', *Quarterly Journal of Economics*, May 1966, pp. 190–207.

Vernon, R., *Manager in the International Economy*, Englewood Cliffs, New Jersey: Prentice-Hall, 1968.

Viner, J., *Canada's Balance of International Indebtedness, 1900–1913*, Cambridge, Mass.: Harvard University Press, 1924.

Wall Street Journal, 'Dollar's Decline Spurs Many Firms to Avoid Deals in Foreign Funds', *Wall Street Journal*, 1st December 1977.

Weston, J. F. and Sorge, B. W., *International Managerial Finance*, Homewood, Illinois: Richard D. Irwing, Inc., 1972.

Willett, T. D. and Forte, F., 'Interest-rate Policy and External Balance', *Quarterly Journal of Economics*, May 1969.

INDEX